European Union and Environmental Governance

Over the past five decades, the European Union (EU) has developed into the most legally and politically authoritative regional organization in the world, wielding significant influence across a wide range of issue areas. *European Union and Environmental Governance* focuses on the growing role of EU environmental and sustainable development policies in Europe and around the world.

Written in a concise and accessible manner, this book introduces and examines the major European and global environmental issues, debates and policies, and provides a critical, evidence-based evaluation of the achievements and shortcomings to date in EU environmental and sustainability governance. Providing both an historical overview and a discussion of the major future legal, political, and economic challenges to the realization of EU goals related to better environmental governance, the authors offer a comprehensive introduction and analysis.

This book is useful reading for students of global environmental politics, comparative environmental politics and policy, international organizations, European politics, and environmental studies.

Henrik Selin is Associate Professor in the Frederick S. Pardee School of Global Studies at Boston University. He conducts research and teaches courses on global and regional politics and policymaking on environment and sustainable development.

Stacy D. VanDeveer is Professor and Department Chair of Political Science at the University of New Hampshire. His research interests include international environmental policymaking and its domestic impacts, the connections between environmental and security issues, the role of expertise in policy making, transatlantic environmental and trade relations and the politics of global commodities markets.

Global Institutions

Edited by Thomas G. Weiss
The CUNY Graduate Center, New York, USA
and Rorden Wilkinson
University of Sussex, Brighton, UK

About the series

The "Global Institutions Series" provides cutting-edge books about many aspects of what we know as "global governance." It emerges from our shared frustrations with the state of available knowledge— electronic and print-wise, for research and teaching—in the area. The series is designed as a resource for those interested in exploring issues of international organization and global governance. And since the first volumes appeared in 2005, we have taken significant strides toward filling conceptual gaps.

The series consists of three related "streams" distinguished by their blue, red, and green covers. The blue volumes, comprising the majority of the books in the series, provide user-friendly and short (usually no more than 50,000 words) but authoritative guides to major global and regional organizations, as well as key issues in the global governance of security, the environment, human rights, poverty, and humanitarian action among others. The books with red covers are designed to present original research and serve as extended and more specialized treatments of issues pertinent for advancing understanding about global governance. And the volumes with green covers—the most recent departure in the series— are comprehensive and accessible accounts of the major theoretical approaches to global governance and international organization.

The books in each of the streams are written by experts in the field, ranging from the most senior and respected authors to first-rate scholars at the beginning of their careers. In combination, the three components of the series—blue, red, and green—serve as key resources for faculty, students, and practitioners alike. The works in the blue and green streams have value as core and complementary readings in courses on, among other things, international organization, global governance, international law, international relations, and international political economy; the red volumes allow further reflection and investigation in these and related areas.

The books in the series also provide a segue to the foundation volume that offers the most comprehensive textbook treatment available dealing with all the major issues, approaches, institutions, and actors in contemporary global governance—our edited work *International Organization and Global Governance* (2014)—a volume to which many of the authors in the series have contributed essays.

Understanding global governance—past, present, and future—is far from a finished journey. The books in this series nonetheless represent significant steps toward a better way of conceiving contemporary problems and issues as well as, hopefully, doing something to improve world order. We value the feedback from our readers and their role in helping shape the on-going development of the series.

A complete list of titles appears at the end of this book. The most recent titles in the series are:

Rising Powers, Global Governance, and Global Ethics (2015)
edited by Jamie Gaskarth

Wartime Origins and the Future United Nations (2015)
edited by Dan Plesch and Thomas G. Weiss

International Judicial Institutions (2nd edition, 2015)
by Richard J. Goldstone and Adam M. Smith

The NGO Challenge for International Relations Theory (2015)
edited by William E. DeMars and Dennis Dijkzeul

21st Century Democracy Promotion in the Americas (2014)
by Jorge Heine and Brigitte Weiffen

BRICS and Coexistence (2014)
edited by Cedric de Coning, Thomas Mandrup, and Liselotte Odgaard

IBSA (2014)
by Oliver Stuenkel

European Union and Environmental Governance

Henrik Selin and Stacy D. VanDeveer

Routledge
Taylor & Francis Group

LONDON AND NEW YORK

First published 2015
by Routledge
2 Park Square, Milton Park, Abingdon, Oxon OX14 4RN

and by Routledge
711 Third Avenue, New York, NY 10017

*Routledge is an imprint of the Taylor & Francis Group, an informa
business*

British Library Cataloguing in Publication Data
A catalogue record for this book is available from the British
Library

Library of Congress Cataloging in Publication Data
Selin, Henrik, 1971-
European Union and environmental governance / Henrik Selin and
Stacy D. VanDeveer.
    pages cm. – (Routledge global institutions series)
Includes bibliographical references and index.
    1. Environmental policy–European Union countries. 2.
Environmental protection–European Union countries. 3.
Sustainable development–Government policy–European Union
countries. I. VanDeveer, Stacy D. II. Title.
    GE190.E85S45 2015
    363.7'0561094–dc23
        2014035035

ISBN: 978-0-415-62881-5 (hbk)
ISBN: 978-0-415-62882-2 (pbk)
ISBN: 978-1-315-72362-4 (ebk)

Typeset in Times New Roman
by Taylor & Francis Books

Contents

Illustrations

Figures

Tables

Boxes

Acknowledgments

This book results from a shared research interest in European environmental affairs, going back to the 1990s. Over the past two decades, we have seen the European Union (EU) grow into a major regional and global force in environmental policymaking. Today's EU is characterized by many impressive accomplishments, even as it faces some daunting challenges. The book is intended for people with varying degrees of understanding and experience of EU politics and inner workings, but who want to learn more about the roles that environmental and sustainable development issues play in the EU. It explains and examines EU environmental governance within broader perspectives of European integration and institution building.

Over the years that we have studied European environmental politics, many people—scholars and practitioners—have contributed to our knowledge and understanding of how the EU works and the ways environmental issues are addressed, through their research, publications, discussions with us, and personal interviews. The list of names of all these people is too long to include here, but we are nevertheless grateful to each and every one of them.

Directly related to the writing of this book, we would like to direct out heartfelt "thank yous" to the series co-editors, Rorden Wilkinson and Thomas Weiss, as well as editorial assistant Martin Burke for their patience, encouragement, and feedback. We are also grateful for two anonymous reviewers, whose insightful suggestions helped to improve the manuscript in several important areas. We have Michael Cole to thank for editing, formatting, and research assistance, while other valuable research assistance came from Tobi Afolayan and Sarah Hill. We thank Noelle Selin for constant support and some technical and design assistance in finalizing illustrations, and Michael Harding for his constant encouragement and occasional food preparation. The hardworking staff at many excellent pubs on both sides of the Atlantic also have our gratitude.

We are thankful for valuable support from our respective institutions, Boston University and the University of New Hampshire. Finally, we extend our thanks to our students. Their piercing questions about what exactly is going on, what theory means, and why the EU matters for environmental governance, forced us to sharpen our thinking and dig deeper into these very interesting but highly complex subjects. We hope that this book adds clarity to some of that.

Henrik Selin and Stacy D. VanDeveer
January 2015

Abbreviations

CAP	Common Agricultural Policy
CEFIC	European Chemical Industry Council
CFP	Common Fisheries Policy
CLP	Classification, labelling and packaging of substances and mixtures
CLRTAP	Convention on Long-range Transboundary Air Pollution
DG	Directorate-General
EAP	Environmental Action Programme
EC	European Community
ECB	European Central Bank
ECC	European Commission
ECHA	European Chemicals Agency
ECSC	European Coal and Steel Community
EEA	European Environment Agency
EEAS	European External Action Service
EEB	European Environmental Bureau
EEC	European Economic Community
EFCA	European Fisheries Control Agency
EFSA	European Food Safety Authority
EFTA	European Free Trade Association
ENP	European Neighbourhood Policy
ETS	Emissions Trading Scheme
EU	European Union
EURATOM	European Atomic Energy Community
GDP	Gross domestic product
GHG	Greenhouse gas
GMO	Genetically modified organism
MEP	Member of the European Parliament
NEC	National Emission Ceiling

OECD	Organisation for Economic Co-operation and Development
PAHs	Polycyclic aromatic hydrocarbons
PM	Particulate matter
REACH	Registration, evaluation, authorisation and restriction of chemicals
REC	Regional Environment Center
RoHS	Restriction on the use of certain hazardous substances in electrical and electronic equipment
SEA	Single European Act
TAC	Total Allowable Catch
UK	United Kingdom
UN	United Nations
UNCCD	United Nations Convention to Combat Desertification
UNCSD	United Nations Commission on Sustainable Development
UNECE	United Nations Economic Commission for Europe
UNEP	United Nations Environment Programme
UNFCCC	United Nations Framework Convention on Climate Change
VOC	Volatile organic compound
WEEE	Waste electrical and electronic equipment
WFD	Water Framework Directive
WTO	World Trade Organization

Introduction

The EU and environmental policy

- **Unity and diversity**
- **EU environmental governance**
- **The state of the European environment**
- **The way forward**

The European Union (EU) is the world's most authoritative international governance system, exercising more influence over its member states than any other international organization. Legally and logistically, the EU is built on a series of foundational treaties negotiated and revised by member states in response to internal and external changes. These treaties outline official authorities of EU bodies, and connections between them, as well as relationships between EU bodies, member states and citizens. They also provide the legal foundation for all EU policymaking. During treaty negotiations, politicians are assumed to pursue both key national interests and expansions of regional cooperation for mutual benefit. Unsurprisingly, long-standing spirited debates persist at both EU and national levels on how to balance these goals appropriately. EU treaty ratification is subject to national-level approval based on domestic legal mandates and political expectations; a given treaty might be voted on by national parliaments in some member states and put to public referendum in others.

Albert Einstein once famously noted, "If at first the idea is not absurd, then there is no hope for it." It took enormous hope and creativity for leading politicians to gaze out over Europe's war-ravaged landscapes after 1945 and imagine the creation of new regional institutions underpinned by jointly accepted treaties supporting peaceful cooperation and economic growth. While a few philosophers and legal scholars long dreamed of secure and free-trading republics guided by the rule of international law on the European continent, this "absurd idea" only gained traction in the wake of World War II's unprecedented destruction and suffering, laying the legal and organizational foundation for what is now the EU.[1] The end of the Cold War in the early 1990s demanded another fundamental reconfiguration of European institutions and public and national interests toward an expanded and more deeply integrated region. European and world politics continue to develop with EU bodies and member states among the most important actors.[2]

Today's EU is characterized by institutional and political complexity, many impressive accomplishments, and a substantial dose of controversy. Dating to the 1957 Rome Treaty on the European Economic Community (EEC) (see Table I.1), the EU has played a significant role in building political stability and managing economic affairs through the world's largest single market (see Box I.1). In 2012, the EU was awarded the Nobel Peace Prize for over six decades of contributions "to the advancement of peace and reconciliation, democracy and human rights in Europe." Yet, Europeans express mixed feelings about the EU and varying combinations of national and European identities.[3] Many countries since 1972 joined after national referendums in support for membership, but a high-profile attempt in the mid-2000s to create a European constitution came to an abrupt halt when it was rejected by voters in France and the Netherlands. Even before this, referendums in Denmark and Ireland in the 1990s and 2000s delayed approval of new treaties and institutional reforms. Voters in Norway have twice (in 1972 and 1994) rejected membership in national campaigns where many leading domestic politicians favored joining.

Box I.1 The single market

The Rome Treaty set a timeline for the original EEC members to create a common market that would abolish national customs barriers within the Community, establish a collective customs union with joint tariffs for imports of goods from outside countries, and develop a common external trade policy, which was achieved on 1 July 1968. To remove remaining physical, technical, and fiscal barriers to free movement, the SEA set out to create a single market where goods, services, capital, and people circulate freely among all member states. This single market, which came into effect on 1 January 1993, is seen as critical both to stimulate economic growth and to ensure that member states' citizens are free to live, work, study, and conduct business anywhere in the EU. However, during recent enlargements, some older member states controversially set time-limited restrictions on the ability of new members' citizens to move to these countries and work. The four members of the European Free Trade Association (EFTA)—Iceland, Norway, Lichtenstein and Switzerland—are also part of the single market, but not the customs union and the external trade policy.

Table I.1 List of EU treaties

Years	Names
Signed 25 March 1957; into force 1 January 1958	The Treaties on the European Economic Community (EEC) and the European Atomic Energy Community (EURATOM) (The Rome Treaties)
Signed 17 and 28 February 1986; into force 1 July 1987	The Single European Act (SEA)
Signed 7 February 1992; into force 1 November 1993	The Treaty on European Union (The Maastricht Treaty)
Signed 2 October 1997; into force 1 May 1999	The Treaty of Amsterdam
Signed 9 December 2000; into force 1 February 2003	The Treaty of Nice
Signed 13 December 2007; into force 1 December 2009	The Treaty of Lisbon

In the 2014 European Parliament elections—with over 350 million eligible voters making it the world's second largest voting process after India's—most of the 43 percent of the electorate who participated voted for pro-EU parties across the ideological spectrum, but several nationalist and anti-immigration parties saw notable success: France's National Front, the Danish People's Party and the UK Independence Party took the most seats in their respective countries. Radical right-wing and left-wing parties also gained ground in Greece, Hungary, Poland, Spain and Sweden. Anti-EU rhetoric can be heard in bars, living rooms, and town squares across Europe. Regulatory attempts by "Brussels" are frequently met by public ridicule as debates break out over the definition of chocolate, the size of bananas, the content of beer, or the legality of Danish pastries. At the same time, public opinion polls show support for many EU initiatives—not least in the environmental area. Data in 2011 showed that 95 percent of respondents across member states felt it was personally important to safeguard the environment, 64 percent believed that environmental policy should be adopted at the regional level, and 89 percent thought that more funding should be allocated towards environmental protection.[4]

This book focuses attention on EU environmental governance—one of the organization's most impactful policy areas—within a broader context of expanded European integration and institution building. It details the emergence of environmental issues on the EU agenda in the early 1970s and traces the legal and political processes through which environmental protection and sustainable development became core goals of the EU, most recently confirmed in the 2009 Lisbon Treaty. It examines the multitude of roles played by EU bodies, member states, organized interest groups and civil society in the regional formulation and domestic implementation of environmental policy. The book also discusses successes and failures of EU policy efforts in different environmental issue areas, the growing role of environmental issues in EU's external relations, and key challenges facing the EU in its ongoing efforts to make more meaningful progress towards sustainability—a central litmus test for the EU's ability to adapt and remain relevant also in the twenty-first century.

Unity and diversity

The EU's partially successful motto—Unity in Diversity—is a rhetorical attempt to bridge gaps between deepening European integration and long-standing aspects of state sovereignty and national identity. Such contradictory issues yield myriad political and economic challenges as even the basic concept of "Europe" is "essentially contested."[5] Europe is often defined as a group of countries located in the same geographical area, as identifiable on a contemporary map. Yet regions are socially constructed and boundaries are fluid over time, influencing debate about what it means to be "European" and where Europe's outer borders lie. Morocco's 1987 membership application was rejected on the grounds that it was not a European country. Later, EU officials went to great lengths to demonstrate that other countries, during their membership application processes in the 1990s and 2000s, were solidly European. Contentious debate continues about whether Turkey is "European enough" to gain membership, or whether Ukrainians and others want to take their countries "closer to Europe."

States joined the EU in different historical contexts, for varying reasons, and with particular interests. Many domestic and international factors shape national views of EU membership, including those related to environmental governance. Initially, there were no official membership requirements, but new members have always had to meet basic democracy criteria; for example, Greece, Portugal and Spain were not invited to join until they had transitioned into democratic political systems. The Copenhagen Criteria, adopted in 1993 and 1995, for the first time outlined three sets of formal criteria to be met by all new members: 1) political criteria such as a stable democracy, rule of law, and protection of human rights and minorities; 2) economic criteria including a functioning market economy and the capacity of domestic actors to cope with competition and market forces within the EU; and 3) legal criteria involving domestic adoption of the full body of joint EU legislation (the so-called "community *acquis*") that applies equally to all member states.

The EU began with six countries in 1958, reaching a total of 28 members with 24 official working languages in 2013 (see Table I.2).[6] While it took almost 30 years to double membership from six to 12, the years 2004 to 2013 saw the addition of 13 new countries. Collectively, over 500 million people, seven percent of all humans, live in EU member states with their own history and political institutions. Europe is also one of the world's most densely populated regions, with 75 percent of people living in urban areas. By 2014, three more candidate countries were engaged in formal membership negotiations (Iceland, Montenegro and Turkey), while three others waited to open such negotiations (Albania, Macedonia and Serbia). Additional Eastern European countries may seek membership at a later date, depending on their domestic political interests and ability to meet the Copenhagen Criteria. Norway, Lichtenstein and Switzerland are also already deeply integrated into the single market and associated EU legislation and may at some point apply for full membership.

The average standard of living in the EU is the envy of much of the world's population, not least the two billion people who survive on less than US$2 dollars a day and lack access to basic education and

Table I.2 EU membership over time, 1958–2013

Year	Members	Total
1958	Belgium, France, Italy, Luxembourg, Netherlands, and West Germany	6
1973	Denmark, Ireland and United Kingdom	9
1981	Greece	10
1986	Portugal and Spain	12
1995	Austria, Finland and Sweden	15
2004	Cyprus, Czech Republic, Estonia, Hungary, Latvia, Lithuania, Malta, Poland, Slovakia and Slovenia	25
2007	Bulgaria and Romania	27
2013	Croatia	28

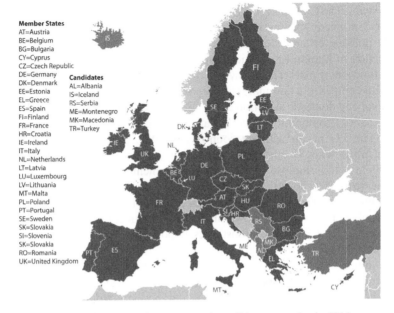

Member States
AT=Austria
BE=Belgium
BG=Bulgaria
CY=Cyprus
CZ=Czech Republic
DE=Germany
DK=Denmark
EE=Estonia
EL=Greece
ES=Spain
FI=Finland
FR=France
HR=Croatia
IE=Ireland
IT=Italy
NL=Netherlands
LT=Latvia
LU=Luxembourg
LV=Lithuania
MT=Malta
PL=Poland
PT=Portugal
SE=Sweden
SK=Slovakia
SI=Slovenia
SK=Slovakia
RO=Romania
UK=United Kingdom

Candidates
AL=Albania
IS=Iceland
RS=Serbia
ME=Montenegro
MK=Macedonia
TR=Turkey

Figure I.1 Map of EU member states and candidate countries in 2014

health-care services. In 2010 the average per capita gross domestic product (GDP) was €24,500, but socioeconomic living conditions across 270 sub-regions were worlds apart.[7] Inner London topped the list of sub-regions with 328 percent of the EU average, or €81,100, followed by Luxembourg (€78,600) and Brussels (€61,300). At the bottom of the list, at 26 percent of the EU average, was Severozapaden, Bulgaria (€2,900), just below Severen tsentralen, Bulgaria (€3,100) and Nord-Est, Romania (€3,600). Of the 68 sub-regions located below the 75 percent level, 63 were located in Eastern and Southern Europe. This economic diversity means that national and local governments and people in different parts of the EU have very different perspectives on environmental policy and its impacts on production, investment, and consumption choices.

EU environmental governance

Europe was the first continent to undergo large-scale industrialization. This helped European countries—and particularly the United Kingdom—grow into global economic powerhouses in the 1800s, including through the aggressive and exploitive use of labor and natural resources in overseas colonies. Since the early 1900s, all EU member states have undergone processes of industrialization and deeper integration into international goods and services markets. This helped lay the economic foundation for the expansive European social welfare states they developed, primarily in the second half of the twentieth century. While European economic and social progress over the past 100 years is truly remarkable, it made the European environment one of the most altered and overused on Earth. Researchers can identify heavy metal pollution not only from the earliest factories in England and Germany, but also from Roman-era mines such as the recently closed mercury mine in Almadén, Spain.[8]

Almost 60 years into EU history, environment and sustainable development issues are a critical part of the regional integration agenda. They help to justify and legitimize growing EU authority, having entered the pantheon of high politics on which the EU "should" act. However, "environment" and "sustainability" are dynamic concepts. Neither term can be defined in a single way that produces quick and widespread agreement about its meaning. They include multifaceted aspects of public health and security, nature/ecological protection, overall quality of life, the rights and needs of future generations (and/or of non-humans), and debates about the kinds of societies, communities, and development people want. What constitutes appropriate action in response to issues like climate change, biodiversity protection, toxics pollution, water management, fisheries depletion, or genetically modified foods—to name only a few—is not easily agreed upon among often complex groups of stakeholders and decision makers.

EU environmental governance involves interactions and decision making among a large number of actors—among them EU bodies, member state national governments, parliaments and regulatory agencies, advocacy groups, and firms—with different interests and perspectives. EU environmental policy dates back to 1972, when the leaders of the then nine EEC member states called for the development of a first Environmental Action Programme (EAP). Since then, European politicians and civil servants have constructed a massive body of environmental law and embarked on quests to transform energy and resource consumption patterns in search of greater sustainability—no small task. Along the way, usual images of environmental politics are displayed, from activists chanting in protest, to scientific reports, student petitions, marketing campaigns for greener products, parliamentary debates, and national leaders arguing and negotiating with one another and championing their accomplishments at podiums in front of an array of brightly colored national flags alongside, since 1986 when it was first flown, the blue and yellow EU flag.

It is not easy to identify exactly how many distinct environmental laws currently exist in the EU. Many larger and smaller policy instruments cut across different policy areas, involving public health, energy, transportation, agriculture, and fisheries, for example, making it difficult clearly to delineate environmental laws from non-environmental laws. Nevertheless, a review by the Institute for European Environmental Policy concluded that over 500 separate policy instruments address major environmental issues.[9] These set ambitious goals and protection standards for people living anywhere in the 28 member states and beyond. They shape choices of politicians, policymakers, investors, product designers, advocates and consumers around the globe. For example, many globally available electronic goods contain fewer hazardous substances and are easier to recycle because of pioneering EU policy impacting outside countries and international markets.[10]

Generally, EU environmental policymaking is driven by six interconnected factors summarized here and illustrated in more detail throughout the book. First, EU environmental law is adopted to address transboundary problems where one member state is affected by industrial and other types of activities in other member states, and is dependent on regulatory actions in these countries to meet its own environmental goals. This is a common situation in many areas of air and water pollution, for example. Such needs for collective action underpin much international environmental cooperation and law making outside Europe as well.

Second, the EU mandates controls on sub-national issues such as bathing water quality or waste water discharges, based on a belief that the EU should set minimum protection standards applicable across all member states to protect people living anywhere in these countries or traveling across national borders within the EU. The increased regulation of such primarily local issues is an important way the EU has moved beyond the scope of most other intergovernmental organizations.

Third, the functioning of the single market necessitates joint environmental policy. The adoption of new environmentally related regulatory requirements and product standards may impede the free exchange of goods and services throughout the single market, demanding harmonization of national measures across all member states. For example, setting pesticide controls, lowering the maximum allowed content of heavy metals such a mercury and cadmium in a particular product, or formulating automobile safety and emissions standards require regional-level policy if fair competition and consumer and environmental protection are to characterize the single market.

Fourth, national policymakers and private sector actors in member states with relatively high environmental regulatory standards often actively seek the adoption of more ambitious standards in other countries with lower requirements to remain economically competitive internationally. They take their policy preferences to Brussels, hoping to use EU bodies and authority to introduce higher, uniform regulations across the single market. This way, all EU firms in the same sector, such as cement or automobile manufacturing, face similar mandates.

Fifth, the sequential adoption of new EU treaties has given EU institutions significantly increased authority on environmental policy formulation over time, meaning that many policymaking powers have been gradually transferred from member states to Brussels. EU bodies often justify their increased engagement by referring to their broad mandate to deepen regional integration, but their efforts to expand EU environmental law are also driven by desires to increase their own influence vis-à-vis national bodies.

Sixth, EU environmental policymaking is shaped by external politics and economic affairs. The EU at times is obligated to develop new regional policy to meet commitments adopted under international environmental agreements, for example. At the same time, EU bodies and member states seek enhanced status and influence by using EU environmental law to shape decisions on, for example, hazardous substances and climate change in other countries and multilateral forums. People in places as diverse as US state capitals, Chinese and Korean energy and environmental ministries, and company boardrooms all over the world closely follow EU law to draw lessons about how emerging standards might shape future policies and investment choices also outside the EU.

The state of the European environment

To assess regional ecological and human health conditions, the EU has produced five comprehensive State of the European Environment reports (in 1994, 1999, 2005, 2010 and 2015) and many more issue-specific and country-focused reports. The 2010 state of the environment report concluded that the 40-year record of EU environmental policy is decidedly mixed.[11] Some environmental policy and management efforts have had real impacts. For example, between 1990 and 2010, the EU-27 achieved significant reductions in regional emissions of major air and water pollutants, including sulfur dioxide (82 percent), chromium (73 percent), arsenic (64 percent), carbon monoxide (62 percent), non-methane volatile organic compounds (56 percent), nitrous oxide (47 percent), and ammonia (28 percent).[12] Furthermore, European greenhouse gas (GHG) emissions have decreased more than those in other industrialized countries since 1990, the region's share of renewable energy sources increased during the same time period, and long-term waste recovery and recycling trends are positive.

At the same time, by 2010 the EU missed its goal on halting biodiversity loss among marine and terrestrial ecosystems, failed to fulfill several emission reduction goals, and did not meet several urban air quality standards despite cuts in key pollutants. EU environmental governance in the mid-2010s is at an important crossroads. On many important environmental and human health issues, the EU struggles to overcome persistent policy implementation problems. On both ecological indicators and environmental politics, significant differences in national conditions and activities exist. All member states' environmental policy implementation records are imperfect, as some national targets and requirements are met while others are missed—sometimes by a wide margin. However, some countries and sub-regions perform better than others. The 2010 state of the environment report furthermore noted that several environmental problems have shifted from being production related to consumption driven. It concluded that European consumption exceeds regional natural resource production by a factor of two, issuing this stern warning:

> Continuing depletion of Europe's stocks of natural capital and flows of ecosystem services will ultimately undermine Europe's economy and erode social cohesion. Most of the negative changes are driven by growing use of natural resources to satisfy production and consumption patterns. The result is a significant environmental footprint in Europe and elsewhere.[13]

Certainly, sustainability is not achieved in Europe; societies and economic activities remain far from any basic idea of sustainable development. Significant shifts in resource use and consumption patterns are needed in all member states if regional sustainability goals are to be achieved. Much improved integration of environmental objectives across other policy areas such as energy, transportation, agriculture, fisheries, industry, trade, and spatial planning is needed. In addition, some reductions in pollution levels stem from a gradual shift of production from Europe to other parts of the world, where goods are then traded back to Europe to be sold on the single market. As such, European consumption patterns and imports remain an important driver of pollution, environmental degradation, and negative human health impacts around the globe.[14]

The way forward

EU politics and the making and implementation of environmental policy are shaped by a great number of institutions and actors—many committed to improved environmental management and human well-being in Europe and around the globe. However, the specific political, economic and administrative means proposed to achieve these broad goals can be highly contested, as EU bodies, member states, stakeholder groups, and individuals hold varying perspectives on how "best" to address specific environmental issues. The subsequent chapters analyze historical and contemporary aspects of EU environmental governance and the continuing search for better environmental protection and much needed greater sustainability. They highlight both successes and shortcomings of EU politics and law to date, and spell out central governance issues facing Europe after four decades of radically expanded regional environmental policymaking.

Chapter 1 looks at European integration and environmental policymaking through the lenses of major theories and conceptual approaches common in EU studies writ large. It discusses theoretical perspectives on environmental issues in EU politics and the appearance of associated ideas of ecological modernization and sustainable development. Chapter 2 examines roles of environmental issues and policy in EU history, tracing their emergence from its early years to the present. The chapter closes with a discussion of sustainability and the challenge of integrating environmental concerns across all areas of EU policymaking.

Chapter 3 outlines the formal mandates of main EU bodies in the development, implementation, and enforcement of environmental policy. It discusses the roles played by lobby groups and civil society in environmental politics and policymaking. Chapter 4 details how environmental policy decisions are made at the EU level and applied across countries, approaching these issues via discussion of oft-used policy stages of agenda setting, policy formulation, implementation, and enforcement.

Chapter 5 discusses nine major cases in EU environmental governance, highlighting the mixed record of accomplishments and continuing challenges in these issue areas. Chapter 6 focuses attention on the EU's active engagement of global, regional and transnational environmental politics beyond its borders, demonstrating the EU's significant influence in Europe and around the world on environmental and sustainability issues. Finally, Chapter 7 discusses three major sets of challenges for the EU in maintaining and expanding its central position in environmental politics in Europe and beyond.

Notes

1 For historical perspectives on European integration, see Derek W. Urwin, *The Community of Europe: A History of European Integration since 1945*, second edn (Harlow: Pearson Education, 1995); John Gillingham, *European Integration, 1950–2003: Superstate or New Market Economy?* (Cambridge: Cambridge University Press, 2003); Desmond Dinan, *Europe Recast: A History of European Union* (Boulder, Col.: Lynne Rienner Publisher, 2004).

2 John McCormick, *Why Europe Matters: The Case for the European Union* (New York: Palgrave Macmillan, 2013).

3 Kaija E. Schilde, "Who are the Europeans? European Identity Outside of European Integration," *Journal of Common Market Studies* 52, no. 3 (2014): 650–67.

4 European Commission, *Special Eurobarometer 365: Attitudes of European Citizens Towards the Environment* (Brussels, 2011).

5 W.B. Gallie, "Essentially Contested Concepts," *Proceedings of the Aristotelian Society* 56 (1956): 167–98.

6 The 24 official EU languages are: Bulgarian, Croatian, Czech, Danish, Dutch, English, Estonian, Finnish, French, German, Greek, Hungarian, Irish, Italian, Latvian, Lithuanian, Maltese, Polish, Portuguese, Romanian, Slovak, Slovene, Spanish and Swedish.

7 See epp.eurostat.ec.europa.eu/cache/ITY_PUBLIC/1-21032013-AP/EN/1-2 1032013-AP-EN.PDF.

8 United Nations Environment Programme, *Global Mercury Assessment* (Geneva: UNEP Chemicals, 2002).

9 See www.europeanenvironmentalpolicy.eu.

10 Henrik Selin, "Minervian Politics and International Chemicals Policy," in *Leadership in Global Institution Building: Minerva's Rule*, ed. Yves Tiberghien (New York: Palgrave Macmillan, 2013), 193–212.

11 European Environment Agency, *The European Environment—State and Outlook 2010* (Copenhagen: European Environment Agency, 2010).

12 European Environment Agency, *European Union Emissions Inventory Report 1990–2010 Under the UNECE Convention on Long-Range Transboundary Air Pollution (LRTAP)* (Luxembourg: Publications Office of the European Union, 2012).

13 European Environment Agency, *The European Environment—State and Outlook 2010*, 9.

14 European Environment Agency, *The European Environment—State and Outlook 2015* (Copenhagen: European Environment Agency, 2015).

1 Theorizing European integration and environmental sustainability

- **Intergovernmentalism**
- **Neo-functionalism**
- **New institutionalism and constructivism**
- **Multilevel governance and Europeanization**
- **The green state and sustainability**

European integration, the surprising growth of the EU, and the greening of EU politics and institutions cannot be properly understood without attending to theory. A large and growing body of academic literature attempts to explain European cooperation shaped by many different initiatives, events, and decisions. It was not inevitable that the twenty-first-century EU of 28 countries would result from the 1950s creation of the EEC by the six founding members. The EU is also a unique entity that is difficult to pigeonhole into traditional conceptualizations of international actors. It does not fit well into standard legal and political categories of sovereign states or international organizations, once having been pointedly described as an "unidentified political object."[1] The EU remains "less" than a traditional nation-state as defined under public international law, lacking the kind of sovereignty and democratic legitimacy claimed by its member states allowing them to act on behalf of their citizens. Yet the EU is much "more" than any other intergovernmental organization anywhere in the world; the legal authority and policymaking powers afforded the EU by its member states is unrivalled among the spectrum of supranational structures in international politics.

Several theories examine EU historical and current complexities, and identify central political drives and significant patterns of political, economic, and social integration across a growing number of European societies. This chapter looks at the multifaceted process of European integration through the lenses of the major theoretical approaches that dominate EU studies—intergovernmentalism, neo-functionalism, new institutionalism and constructivism, and multilevel governance and Europeanization. Some of these rely primarily on agent-centered approaches, while others apply more structurally focused perspectives.[2] Importantly, the different theories are neither mutually exclusive, nor collectively exhaustive of ways to view European politics and policy-making. Furthermore, no single perspective is objectively the best at explaining all aspects of such a multifaceted empirical case as EU development over six decades. In addition, this chapter discusses conceptual perspectives on the changing roles of environmental issues in national and international politics and the emergence of related ideas of ecological modernization and sustainable development.

Intergovernmentalism

Influential in many studies of international politics, intergovernmentalist theories draw on agent-based, rational actor conceptions of policy-making. In such studies, the nation-state remains the central unit of analysis.[3] States are seen as the primary actors in international policy-making, characterized as acting in calculated pursuit of their own basic interests stemming from statehood. Issue-specific interests are formulated primarily through domestic political processes, and are typically seen as centering on efforts to secure national influence and benefits vis-à-vis other countries in international forums. Here it is argued that a strict protection of national interest often makes it difficult to reach commonly acceptable solutions, especially against the preferences of larger countries. Furthermore, intergovernmentalist theories do not believe that international organizations affect the basic characteristics of multilateral politics and policymaking. Instead, such organizations merely reflect the basic distribution of power among their member states, serving as a tool states use when they so desire.

Applied to the EU going back to the 1960s, intergovernmentalism draws attention to high-level member state interactions among national political leaders, including during treaty negotiations, for driving major policy developments.[4] These traditional political processes are seen as critical to the medium- and long-term directions of the EU, as national governments seek to retain sovereignty and control over many European policy developments even as they agree to expand some supranational structures. Thus, intergovernmentalists often focus less on what has changed in EU institution building, in terms of the expanded numbers and roles of EU bodies, and more on what remains (more or less) the same: states' habitual pursuit of their defined national interests and the continuing attempts of the most powerful ones to retain influence over international organizations and collective policymaking. Intergovernmentalist analysis proves particularly valuable in drawing attention to the importance of national interests and strategies, and for explaining where, when and under what circumstances states are reluctant to pool sovereign authority or resist particular aspects of European integration.

By the 1990s, a more recent conception of liberal intergovernmentalism shaped much EU analysis.[5] In this framework of analysis, self-interested state leaders are first seen to develop an understanding of their national interests, and then articulate these preferences through intergovernmental bargaining. Neither national interests nor bargaining processes are thought to be much influenced by EU bodies. Rather, outcomes of inter-state negotiations are determined mostly by bargaining power, deal making, and side payments. Crucially, liberal intergovernmentalism views EU bodies as vehicles by which agreed-upon commitments are made more credible and secure than those in many weaker international forums. In instances where states voluntarily agree to pool authority, they do so because the preferences of more powerful states converge and deals are struck to bring along less powerful (and therefore less influential) states skeptical of proposed policy changes.

As ecological issues became a common topic of discussion among heads of state and national governments, intergovernmentalist approaches expanded into the area of environmental politics. Here, the basic assumptions of state interest formulation and state interaction remain the same as in other policy areas where intergovernmentalist perspectives are applied. Thus, intergovernmentalist studies view major EU environmental policy goals as the result of state-driven initiatives and outcomes of state-centric bargaining processes. In support of such an intergovernmentalist approach, scholars working in this tradition often point to decisions by European heads of state and governments on the adoption of Sustainable Development Strategies in 2001 and 2006, or their collective commitment to the climate and energy packages in 2009 and 2014 as examples of high-level political processes shaping policy outcomes based on a convergence of national interests. As such, they typically highlight instances when national political leaders come together to shape EU environmental politics by expressing policy preferences based on domestic conditions and existing national policies.

Intergovernmentalist studies argue that EU member states, despite deepening European integration over decades, have deliberately maintained significant influence over regional environmental policymaking, as EU bodies gained decision-making authority. As the most influential states' interests converge around power plant emissions standards, for example, they use EU forums to build and implement credible policies in support of these shared national interests. Related to this, green leader states with relatively high domestic environmental standards may seek to "trade up" their national policies to the European level through the adoption of more ambitious, harmonized EU standards.[6] In contrast, member states with lower (or non-existent) mandates may seek to slow down the development of new environmental policies. National governments strive to minimize implementation costs, as they compete for the adoption of regional policies that conform best to their domestic structures.[7] Such "leader-laggard" dynamics, where states are seen to act rationally based on national interests and conditions, are also examined in Europeanization studies (discussed below).

Neo-functionalism

Neo-functionalist theories have been applied to study of EU institution building since the 1950s, as scholarly debates in the early decades of European cooperation were characterized primarily by discussions between intergovernmentalist and neo-functionalist explanations of forces driving deepening integration. Combining claims and insights mainly from the international relations and political science literatures, neo-functionalist theories argue that collaborative governance arrangements are created out of basic and functional needs of societies to coordinate decisions and help solve collective problems, such as environmental degradation and public health risks.[8] From this perspective, international organizations are created by states to fulfill practical functions, and given specific mandates guiding their activities. Neo-functionalists often argue that without some kind of governance mechanism, important collective (public) goods will not be adequately provided as countries are functionally interdependent. Compared to intergovernmentalist theories, neo-functionalist perspectives to a much greater extent highlight the influence of EU bodies operating alongside states in regional politics.

A key assertion in neo-functionalist theories is that technical and political decisions to cooperate in one area may have significant influence on subsequent handling of other issues. For example, the early decision by the six founding countries of the EEC to share governance of coal and steel production served as a critical basis for future collective decisions to share authority over other sectors and issues. While intergovernmentalists stress the importance of high-level interaction between heads of states and governments in shaping regional policy agendas and outcomes, neo-functionalist explanations focus more on lower-level, day-to-day operations and experiences for slowly solidifying and deepening integration over time. Early neo-functionalists often argued that subsequent pressures pushing greater integration were largely unintended and unforeseen consequences of "functional spillover" from earlier decisions.[9] Later analysts stress that "political spillover" is frequently driven by EU bodies, calling for greater integration and more EU-wide policy to address issues of common concern, believing these are best addressed regionally.[10]

Consequently, whereas intergovernmentalists view many EU policy outcomes as the result of carefully calculated and strategic choices by member states, neo-functionalist explanations often assume a lower degree of rational choice and a more limited ability by national governments to steer specific processes and determine outcomes. From this perspective, many environmental policy decisions cannot be anticipated by simply reviewing the interests of the most powerful states and trying to estimate their willingness to engage in limited compromise. Rather, neo-functionalists stress that many processes and decisions contributing to deepening European integration occur outside the control of individual countries. Furthermore, neo-functionalists argue that as member states, EU bodies, and advocacy groups learn to cooperate over time, and see the resulting benefits, this can significantly impact institution building by making collaboration the normatively preferred response to future problems. Decision making might start around "low-level" technical concerns, but is often expanded into institution building on "high-level" issues.

Neo-functionalist analyses of European integration often pay more attention to environmental issues than do intergovernmentalist studies. In many ways, neo-functionalist perspectives offer attractive explanations for the vast expansion of individual EU environmental policy instruments since the late 1960s, as such studies often focus on activities and political drivers outside European summits and other top-level forums. Many environmental issues relate to a central concern of the EU project—the creation and operation of the single market. However, related regional collaboration often started around technical issues largely out of public view and of little interest to state leaders, such as the development of joint standards for harmonized risk assessments of pesticides, industrial chemicals and heavy metals. Over time, progress on these shared systems of information gathering, assessment, and measurement were used by supportive EU actors as a platform for legitimizing expanded cooperation on more explicitly political issues such the regulation of specific substances.

Neo-functionalist theories embrace the idea that many different European actors shape EU environmental agenda setting and policymaking. They often stress the political and organizational complexity through which policies are negotiated and implemented. On the environmental policymaking side, the formulation of many laws on, for example, air and water pollution or chemicals management have been greatly impacted by previously adopted decisions and the opinions of EU bodies and large stakeholder groups (e.g. subject to functional and political spillovers). With respect to the implementation of major environmental policies on chemicals management and genetically modified organisms (GMOs), smaller committees with members from EU bodies and national governments exercise considerable influence over narrow rule making. These decisions are sometimes described as "technical," but can have far-reaching political consequences for private sector actors' obligations and national authorities' ability to operate under existing environmental law.

New institutionalism and constructivism

In the 1970s, many social science and humanities disciplines began paying greater attention to the influence of institutions—just as European cooperation and environmental policymaking accelerated as member states initiated revisions to the original Rome Treaty.[11] This theoretical turn towards "new institutionalism" developed into several variants, attempting to explain the many ways institutions "matter," including in Europe. In common, new institutionalism theories examine how informal social structures consisting of particular norms, rules, and decision-making practices and more formalized organizations and bodies shape individual actors' behavior on environmental issues and other policy fields.[12] New institutionalism also stipulates that actors' interests and preferences are at least partly shaped through social interaction; institutions, to a much higher degree than assumed in intergovernmentalism, shape what different actors regard as appropriate and legitimate behavior, thereby having direct influence on environmental policy debates and decisions.

Within new institutionalism, rational choice approaches examine how a collective governance system, or a separate organization, shapes the incentives, preferences, and decisions of individual decision makers. While intergovernmentalist theories see national interest formation as a result of mainly domestic factors, rational institutionalist studies of the EU may, for example, seek to understand how external formal rule changes in relationships between EU bodies affect their behavior and positions, and how these events impact efforts by member states and others to formulate environmental policy.[13] Historical institutionalism argues that both formal and informal EU institutions, once established, come to shape their creators and other participants not just by changing specific incentives impacting individual choices, but also by more fundamentally altering actors' interests and shaping their long-term expectations about how different environmental and sustainability issues should be addressed at the regional level.[14] In addition, institutionalists of all stripes tend to see the gradually growing authority of EU bodies on environmental and other issues as both a cause and an outcome of deepening European integration.

Institutionalist theories point out that EU environmental laws and practices shaping integration get institutionalized over time, helping to secure their continued existence and influence. Member state governments and their interests evolve over time, including as a result of national elections or shifts in public opinion, but the activities and choices of a member state government at any given time are constrained by existing European agreements and policies, as these cannot simply be renegotiated every time national interests or governments change. Furthermore, EU laws and bodies are seen to create path dependencies, and actors may seek to sustain these path dependencies when they believe doing so serves their interests. In contrast to neofunctionalist theories that often view integration processes as changeable and difficult to predict, path dependency perspectives stress that an environmental policy decision on, for example, air quality standards can limit the range of future possible decisions as policy processes unfold. At the same time, national governments are often unable to control events or specific environmental policy outcomes.

Like new institutionalism, constructivist theories gaining prominence in the 1990s examine how political actors formulate their interests and engage in cooperation.[15] Constructivists add to the other theories by more deeply studying how both institutions and actors' interests are molded—or "socially constructed"—through social interaction, often focusing on the importance of ideas and discourses.[16] While rationalist approaches see actors' interests on environmental and other issues as strategically formulated, constructivists seek to understand the more complex ways preferences and choices are shaped by a variety of social factors. In contrast to intergovernmentalists, who portray EU member states as simply trying to maximize their own gains, constructivists examine how member states perceive themselves and others and how such perceptions—and other actors and structures—influence the way they interact and formulate environmental policy. In this respect, constructivists believe that the EU more profoundly shapes preferences and deeper identities of member states and other actors engaged in European environmental policymaking and implementation, than do many institutionalist theories.

For constructivists, EU institution building has contributed to a gradual change in the identities of member states, EU bodies, other organizations, and involved individuals. Operating within a set of socially constructed institutions and taking on socially constructed roles, constructivists argue that EU policy actors seek to formulate "appropriate" policy responses to specific environmental problems. What is collectively seen as an appropriate policy solution to, for example, climate change or biodiversity loss can be significantly influenced by non-material ideas and social forces, which are given less prominence in the earlier theories. Importantly, for constructivists, actors' identities, values, and preferences are not fixed, but are continually reconstituted through social interaction and may also change significantly over time. European political actors' preferences are sometimes altered in support of the idea that European policy solutions are more appropriate and effective than nationally focused initiatives and responses. Many EU actors have come to believe, for example, that it is often "better" to formulate environmental policy at the regional level than separately within each member state.

Multilevel governance and Europeanization

As the EU gained greater legal authority through the treaty revisions and became more influential in European politics, analysts in the 1990s began developing new analytical frameworks to study structures and dynamics of regional integration. The concept of multilevel governance originates within EU analyses, though subsequently applied to other regions and global governance. Multilevel governance studies challenge the notion common in intergovernmentalist and other theories that European nation-states are not affected by integration in any deeper way, as they shift focus away from state-centric governance. Instead, analysts pay closer attention to the ways policy-making authority is shared among many different actors across sub-national, national, and supranational levels.[17] Consequently, such analyses focus on how European politics and policymaking are linked (or not) within and across governance scales, and how the allocation of formal and informal decision-making powers changes over time, impacting roles of public authorities and traditional conceptions of state sovereignty.

Multilevel governance studies is connected to long-standing analyses of policymaking in federal political systems, such as those in the United

States or Germany.[18] As these examine how governance efforts and authority are dispersed across organizational scales and forums, many environmental issues are well suited for such research. Multilevel governance studies centering on vertical connections may examine how actors involved in, for example, climate change and energy policy are connected across regional, national, and local levels—such policy is currently debated and enacted in forums ranging from global summits and EU bodies to national governments, city halls, small businesses, and campuses. These studies highlight that as substantial authority over climate change and energy policy shifted from the national to the EU level over 20 years, the political action, investments and coordination challenges involved in these policy areas play out at every level of social organization. Similarly, multilevel governance studies examine how water and fisheries management and biodiversity protection involve many complex interactions from high-level EU meetings to local communities and individuals.

Alongside multilevel governance studies, scholars have paid growing attention to Europeanization processes in the context of expanding regional cooperation and institution building. Rather diverse in nature, Europeanization approaches examine drivers and impacts of EU political, economic, and social integration and policymaking across an increasing number of countries.[19] Because EU environmental policy has grown rapidly in scope and authority compared to many other major policy areas, it is the subject of considerable Europeanization research. Importantly, analysts use the term Europeanization to describe and investigate several different political processes. These include the ways the EU exerts top-down influence on member states, the expansion of EU-level accumulation of policy authority and competences, the growing importance of the EU as a political reference point for national and sub-national actors, the horizontal transfer of concepts and policies between member states, and two-way interactions between member states and the EU.[20] These conceptualizations of Europeanization processes are not only different in character, but may be more or less applicable in individual cases of environmental politics.

Viewing Europeanization from a top-down perspective as the EU gains greater authority, new policies are transferred down to member states responsible for implementation. For example, research about why and how countries in Central, Eastern and Southern Europe adopted the massive body of EU environmental law as part of their accession negotiations starting in the 1990s often takes a top-down perspective, since these member states did not participate in the making of the earlier policies.[21] Such work may take a rationalist approach to understanding how EU bodies demand or induce domestic adjustments via changes in incentives, or it may draw on constructivist approaches to explore how changes in domestic political actors' beliefs and preferences influence national or sub-national decision making.[22] Top-down focused studies also examine how specific EU environmental laws are transposed into national law in member states. Much of this literature finds that the EU drives substantial institutional change within member states, but this often does not result in uniformity across member states. Policy ideas and initiatives may also diffuse between member states.[23]

Related to multilevel governance approaches, studies of the Europeanization of environmental policy examine two-way interactions between member states and EU bodies. Some look at member state strategies in their interactions with each other and the EU, including being pace setters, foot draggers, or fence sitters (then sometimes overlapping with intergovernmentalist approaches).[24] Pace setters seek to shape European policies based on domestic preferences as they engage with, and seek support from, EU bodies. These states may strive to coordinate efforts to fight cross-boundary pollution, to protect domestic industries subject to relatively stringent mandates, or have an interest in expanding technology markets for their own exporting firms, via EU policy making. Also, governments of high-regulating states may respond to "green" domestic demands. Multinational firms often support harmonization too, especially if based in high regulation states, preferring to comply with only one set of EU rules rather than a diverse set of national standards.

In contrast, foot draggers aim to contain attempts by other member states and EU bodies to set higher standards. Their less demanding national environmental regulations may constitute a competitive advantage over competitors in other countries. In such instances, the formulation of stricter EU standards provides no new sales opportunities for their industries, while they may need to import abatement technology from foreign firms. Foot draggers also view building regulatory structures for new EU laws as expensive, often feeling little political pressure from domestic environmental advocacy groups. In between the pace setters and the foot draggers, member states may adopt a passive fence-sitting strategy when they do not give much importance to a specific environmental issue, or when they do not anticipate significant implementation costs. (However, they may miscalculate the costs of domestic adjustments.) National governments may also allow the EU to adopt environmental policies, which they were not able to formulate at home in the face of domestic opposition, allowing them to conveniently "blame Brussels."

The green state and sustainability

In addition to theoretical diversity in the study of European cooperation and integration processes, different perspectives exist on issues of
European regional and national environmental policy development, sustainable development, and ecological modernization. Certainly, a general "greening" of states across the industrialized world has occurred
over the last 40 years.[25] Four broad trends are discernible: 1) an enormous
expansion of the environmental domain covering a larger number of
policy issues and management efforts; 2) a deepening of state engagement with environmental issues as these are increasingly integrated into
different sectors and programs; 3) environmental management has
become central to state activities and structures and is now seen as
important for welfare and security issues more broadly; and 4) the
environment has developed into a permanent area of political conten-
tion where public, private, and civil society actors cooperate and
compete for authority and influence.[26]

Connected to these four trends, many European efforts to green the
state from the 1960s to the 1980s focused on establishing public organizations and administrative capacities for environmental policymaking,
implementation, assessment, and enforcement. During this time many
reactive and media-specific policies were introduced, focusing on reducing air and water emissions of particular pollutants as by-products of
industrialization. Since the 1980s, the EU's more ambitious policy
agenda of integrated environmental management across sources and
sectors has sought a broader transformation of societal and commercial activities so that these have less adverse ecological impacts. As a
result, a nascent "environmental state" has taken its place among other
central state functions, including offering basic security (related to
internal order and external threats), stimulating economic growth and
prosperity, and providing the many social services associated with the
modern welfare state in Europe.[27]

The close connection between environment and economics has long
been visible in the construction and protection of the single market and
the maintenance of fair and open competition among member state
firms and workers.[28] In fact, the priority given by European political
leaders to economic development and integration, and the prosperity
and peace it was believed to produce, was among the most important
impetus for the early growth of EU environmental debates and policies
(as well as a reason for giving more legal authority on environmental issues
and regulation to EU bodies). For example, if cars are to be sold all over
Europe without tariffs and other forms of trade barriers in a single

market, then such a market will need some form of common environmental vehicle standards to ensure compatibility across countries (emission controls, fuel content, etc.). Or, if air pollution damage to the environment and human health from power plants and manufacturing industries is to be reduced in ways that do not discriminate against firms in particular countries or inhibit the functioning of the single market, emissions in many cases need to be regulated at the regional level.

Frequently EU environmental policymaking is explicitly linked with a political commitment to the modern welfare state, with analysts pointing out that Europeans are used to paying relatively high income taxes and other fees for the security afforded by the welfare state.[29] Thus, they argue that Europeans are comparatively willing to absorb costs associated with GHG reductions and other measures to avoid, or at least limit, adverse ecological impacts on current and future generations in support of building a "green welfare state."[30] Further, EU environmental policy is grounded on the precautionary principle as a means for minimizing hazards, including with respect to climate change mitigation. This is consistent particularly with social-democratic policies creating broad social safety nets based on a desire to reduce risks to individuals and communities, but related ideas have now become thoroughly politically mainstream and institutionalized across the EU. This, however, does not mean that Europeans are always more precautionary than people in other parts of the world, or that EU environmental policy is constantly taking a more precautionary stand as compared with other countries' policy measures.[31]

As the concept of sustainable development gained prominence, the Maastricht Treaty made it a legally binding goal for the EU in the early 1990s. In its most basic sense, this means that environmental concerns and management should be integrated with social and economic development strategies in all areas of EU activity. EU sustainability issues were further discussed in the 2001 Sustainable Development Strategy, most recently reviewed in 2009, and sustainable development remains a fundamental objective for the EU under the Lisbon Treaty.[32] Importantly, dominant "weak" versions of sustainable development do not challenge the operation of current capitalist systems for production and consumption at any deeper level; EU sustainable development commitments involve a political effort to green market-based capitalism in Europe in the twenty-first century, not overthrow it.[33] Thus, EU environmental policy is currently developed and implemented alongside other high-level political initiatives to make Europe—its countries, firms, and workers—more flexible and economically competitive in expanding regional and global markets.

Consistent with EU definitions of sustainable development and associated policy efforts, as well as a continued commitment to neo-liberal economic principles, the concept of ecological modernization (as an outgrowth of modernization theory) has gained increasing traction since the 1980s.[34] This concept stresses the importance of the ability and adaptability of societies to address both minor and major ecological challenges as countries continue to develop economically and socially. Early discussions of ecological modernization processes highlighted the importance of technological innovation, arguing that many production-related environmental problems such as different forms of pollution could be addressed largely through the development and use of more advanced technologies. Subsequent work continued to recognize the importance of technological change, but accentuated the importance of economic structural change. In this context, public authorities were given an important role in reformulating broader rules and changing incentives for firms and individuals to alter their behavior through the introduction of new policy instruments and legal mandates.[35] Similar ideas are central to recent "green economy" debates.[36]

In line with notions of ecological modernization and a green economy transition, a contemporary dominating discourse in Europe (and other parts of the industrialized world) is that a shift towards sustainability is not just about introducing costly restrictions on harmful activities. Rather, sustainability changes are seen to offer new economic and social opportunities for improving quality of life for people living anywhere in the EU. Not only is there not an inherent conflict between expanded environmental protection and continued economic growth, but these two goals are often described as mutually supportive and collectively achievable. In this vein, statements by EU bodies and member states that greening economies and energy systems to reduce emissions of carbon dioxide and other pollutants can simultaneously create new jobs and open up economic opportunities for new industries and stimulate technological innovations are broadly consistent with ecological modernization ideas. In addition, such thought supports more use of voluntary and market-based environmental policy instruments, along with a continued strong role for the state. Assumptions and beliefs associated with ecological modernization are now so common among EU political actors and documents that it is difficult to over-estimate their importance, even if the concept itself is not always explicitly mentioned.

Some analysts and environmental activists, however, have criticized EU conceptualizations of sustainable development and ecological modernization as too timid. Common in all industrialized countries, they see them as a set of weak ideas that may engender political and economic reforms, but offer few genuine paths toward the structural reshaping of governance and economic activities required to achieve greater—and necessary—European and global sustainability. Many of these critiques focus on the need for societies and individuals to embrace a "strong" version of sustainability and greener values, fundamentally altering existing production and consumption patterns to have any chance to stay within local, national, and planetary ecological boundaries.[37] Irrespective of whether such alternative arguments and perspectives are taken seriously, it is clear, as stated in the 2010 State of the European Environment Report, that the EU has a long way to go before it can make legitimate claims about having fulfilled most of its stated environmental policy goals and reached a meaningful form of sustainability.

Notes

1 Vivien A. Schmidt, "The European Union: Democratic Legitimacy in a Regional State?" *Journal of Common Market Studies* 42, no. 5 (2004): 975–97.
2 Mark A. Pollack, "Theorizing EU Policy-Making," in *Policy-Making in the European Union*, ed. Helen Wallace, Mark A. Pollack and Alasdair R. Young (Oxford: Oxford University Press, 2010), 15–44.
3 Stanley Hoffman, "Obstinate or Obsolete? The Fate of the Nation-State and the Case of Western Europe," *Daedalus* 95, no. 3 (1966): 862–915.
4 Andrew Moravcsik, "Negotiating the Single European Act: National Interests and Conventional Statecraft in the European Community," *International Organization* 45, no. 1 (1991): 19–56.
5 Andrew Moravcsik, "Preferences and Power in the European Community: A Liberal Intergovernmentalist Approach," *Journal of Common Market Studies* 31, no. 4 (1993): 473–524.
6 David Vogel, *Trading Up: Consumer and Environmental Regulation in a Global Economy* (Cambridge, Mass.: Harvard University Press, 1995).
7 Duncan Liefferink and Mikael Skou Andersen, "Strategies of the 'Green' Member States in EU Environmental Policy-making," *Journal of European Public Policy* 5, no. 2 (1998): 254–27; Martin Jänicke, "Trend-Setters in Environmental Policy: The Character and Role of Pioneer Countries," *European Environment* 15, no. 2 (2005): 129–42.
8 Ernst B. Haas, *The Uniting of Europe: Political, Social, and Economic Forces 1950–1957* (Stanford, Calif.: Stanford University Press, 1958).
9 Leon N. Lindberg, *The Political Dynamics of European Economic Integration* (Stanford, Calif.: Stanford University Press, 1963).
10 Stephen George, *Politics and Policy in the European Community*, second edn (Oxford: Oxford University Press, 1991).
11 John W. Meyer and Brian Rowan, "Institutionalized Organizations: Formal Structure as Myth and Ceremony," *American Journal of Sociology* 83, no. 2 (1977): 340–63; James G. March and Johan P. Olsen, "The New Institutionalism: Organizational Factors in Political Life," *American Political Science Review* 78, no. 3 (1984): 734–49.

12 James G. March and Johan P. Olsen, *Rediscovering Institutions: The Organizational Basis of Politics* (New York: The Free Press, 1989); Walter W. Powell and Paul J. DiMaggio, eds, *The New Institutionalism in Organizational Analysis* (Chicago, Ill.: University of Chicago Press, 1991).

13 Fritz W. Scharpf, "The Joint-Decision Trap: Lessons from German Federalism and European Integration," *Public Administration* 66, no. 3 (1988): 239–78.

14 Peter A. Hall, *Governing the Economy: The Politics of State Intervention in Britain and France* (Oxford: Oxford University Press, 1986).

15 Alexander Wendt, "Anarchy is What States Make of it: The Social Construction of Power Politics," *International Organization* 46, no. 2 (1992): 391–425; Alexander Wendt, *Social Theory of International Politics* (Cambridge: Cambridge University Press, 1999).

16 Vivien A. Schmidt, "Discursive Institutionalism: The Explanatory Power of Ideas and Discourse," *Annual Review of Political Science* 11 (2008): 303–26.

17 Gary Marks, Liesbet Hooghe and Kermit Blank, "European Integration from the 1980s: State-Centric v. Multi-Level Governance," *Journal of Common Market Studies* 34, no. 3 (1996): 341–78; Liesbet Hooghe and Gary Marks, *Multi-Level Governance and European Integration* (Lanham, Md.: Rowman and Littlefield, 2001).

18 Henrik Selin and Stacy D. VanDeveer, "Federalism, Multilevel Governance, and Climate Change Politics across the Atlantic," in *Comparative Environmental Politics*, ed. Paul F. Steinberg and Stacy D. VanDeveer (Cambridge, Mass.: MIT Press, 2012), 341–68.

19 Yves Mény, Pierre Muller and Jean-Louis Quermonne, eds, *Adjusting to Europe: The Impact of the European Union on National Institutions and Policies* (London: Routledge, 1996); Christoph Knill, *The Europeanisation of National Administrations: Patterns of Institutional Change and Persistence* (Cambridge: Cambridge University Press, 2001).

20 Andrew Jordan and Duncan Liefferink, eds, *Environmental Policy in Europe: The Europeanization of National Environmental Policy* (New York: Routledge, 2005).

21 Joann Carmine and Stacy D. VanDeveer, eds, *EU Enlargement and the Environment: Institutional Change and Environmental Policy in Central and Eastern Europe* (New York: Routledge, 2005).

22 David Vogel, *The Politics of Precaution: Regulating Health, Safety, and Environmental Risks in Europe and the United States* (Princeton, N.J.: Princeton University Press, 2012).

23 Duncan Liefferink and Andrew Jordan, "An 'Ever Closer Union' of National Policy? The Convergence of National Policy in the European Union," *European Environment* 15, no. 2 (2005): 102–13.

24 Tanja A. Börzel, "Pace-Setting, Foot-dragging and Fence-sitting: Member State Responses to Europeanization," *Journal of Common Market Studies* 40, no. 2 (2002): 193–214.

25 John S. Dryzek, Christian Hunold and David Schlosberg, with David Downes and Hans-Kristian Hernes, "Environmental Transformation of the State: the USA, Norway, Germany and the UK," *Political Studies* 50, no. 4 (2002): 659–82.

26 James Meadowcroft, "Greening the State?" in *Comparative Environmental Politics*, ed. Paul F. Steinberg and Stacy D. VanDeveer (Cambridge, Mass.: MIT Press, 2012), 63–87.

27 Meadowcroft, "Greening the State?"
28 Henrik Selin and Stacy D. VanDeveer, "Politics of Trade and Environment in the European Union," in *Handbook on Trade and Environment*, ed. K.P. Gallagher (Aldershot: Edward Elgar, 2008), 194–203.
29 John R. Schmidt, "Why Europe Leads on Climate Change," *Survival* 50, no. 4 (2008): 83–96.
30 Lennart Lundqvist, *Sweden and Ecological Governance: Straddling the Fence* (Manchester: Manchester University Press, 2004).
31 Vogel, *The Politics of Precaution*, 2012.
32 Council of the European Union, *2009 Review of the EU Sustainable Development Strategy—Presidency Report* (Brussels, 1 December, 2009); Maria Lee. *EU Environmental Law, Governance and Decision-Making*, second edn (Oxford: Hart Publishing, 2014).
33 Harriet Bulkeley, Andrew Jordan, Richard Perkins and Henrik Selin, "Governing Sustainability: Rio+20 and the Road Beyond," *Environment & Planning C: Government & Policy* 31, no. 6 (2013): 958–70.
34 Arthur P.J. Mol, *Globalization and Environmental Reform: The Ecological Modernization of the Global Economy* (Cambridge, Mass.: MIT Press, 2001).
35 Joseph Murphy, "Ecological Modernisation," *Geoforum* 31, no. 1 (2000): 1–8.
36 Olivia Bina, "The Green Economy and Sustainable Development: An Uneasy Balance?" *Environment & Planning C: Government & Policy* 31, no. 6 (2013): 1023–47.
37 John Dryzek, *The Politics of Earth: Environmental Discourses*, second edn (Oxford: Oxford University Press, 2005); Thomas Princen, *The Logic of Sufficiency* (Cambridge, Mass.: MIT Press, 2005).

2 EU history and the environment

- **From Rome, via Stockholm, to Paris**
- **From Paris to Brussels**
- **The Single European Act and the environment**
- **Maastricht and the EU**
- **From Amsterdam to Lisbon and beyond**
- **Sustainable development, economic growth and policy integration**

The EU has defied many dire predictions of its demise and surprised skeptics by moving toward much greater economic and political integration. Nevertheless, European institution building is a complicated process where political challenges force occasional course corrections and reevaluation by political leaders and citizens. Environmental issues were not central drivers of early European integration; security, economics and social welfare were typically more influential. Yet, environmental politics have been integral to European regionalism for over four decades.[1] While the total number of EU environmental laws has grown steadily since the 1970s, not every new environmental policy instrument increases the total number of EU laws. Large sets of recent environmental legislation—on air pollution, water quality and hazardous substances, for example—replaced multiple pieces of older law, in effect reducing the overall number of environmental laws as they expanded coverage and raised standards. Thus, "how much" environmental law exists is not simply a matter of how many laws are on the books at a given time, but also about the stringency, scope and clarity of law.[2]

The body and the level of ambition of EU environmental law have increased greatly, with especially rapid policy developments taking place in the 1990s and early 2000s. This chapter provides an overview of EU history with a focus on environmental governance. It summarizes the basic treaties on which the EU is based and built, examines relationships between these treaties and environmental politics and policymaking, and discusses a number of important membership enlargements and institutional developments related to environmental decision making. The chapter starts with the 1950s creation of the Rome Treaty, moving chronologically through to the Lisbon Treaty. It ends with discussion of the EU Sustainable Development Strategy and central challenges facing the EU and its member states in the persistent struggle to set, implement, and meet ambitious goals related to environmental and human health protection and sustainability.

From Rome, via Stockholm, to Paris

Since the late 1940s, European integration and expanding political, economic and social interdependence have been driven by a complex set of factors. These efforts also received substantial backing from the International Bank for Reconstruction and Development (as part of the World Bank) and the US Marshall Plan. A combination of political and economic ideas lay behind the early post-World War II initiative to integrate primarily Franco–German coal and steel production—two raw materials critical to both countries' industrial and military power. These ideas were presented in the 1950 Schuman plan, named after the French Foreign Minister Robert Schuman. Jean Monnet, a French political economist and diplomat who drafted much of the plan, is often regarded as a chief architect of European integration. Schuman, in a related declaration supporting deepening European integration, stated that the goal was to make any war between the two historical antagonists France and Germany "not merely unthinkable, but materially impossible."

The French integration proposal was met with strong support by the West German Chancellor Konrad Adenauer, who shared the desire to rebuild a peaceful and stable Europe. This was generally consistent with broader domestic political interests in West Germany, which included security-related efforts to reconnect with the United States and other countries through membership in the North Atlantic Treaty Organization, as the Cold War accelerated. This dual track of security and economic cooperation by Germany and other European countries aimed to reduce the likelihood of armed conflict and promote shared prosperity. As a precursor to the current EU, Belgium, France, Italy, Luxembourg, Netherlands, and West Germany, following a proposal in the Schuman Declaration, signed the Paris Treaty in 1951, creating the European Coal and Steel Community pooling national production capabilities. The same six European countries went on to negotiate two

1957 Rome treaties, forming the EEC and the European Atomic Energy Community (EURATOM), respectively. The three treaties collectively establish three communities, which existed simultaneously. The EU's legal basis still ultimately rests on the EEC treaty, amended five times over the subsequent 50 years.

The EEC initially developed alongside the EFTA, another Western European organization which became operational in 1960. EFTA started with seven countries: Austria, Denmark, Norway, Portugal, Sweden, Switzerland, and the UK. Whereas the EEC sought to expand both political and economic cooperation, EFTA had a narrower focus on free trade and economic integration. EFTA also lacked a common external customs tariff. The balance between the EEC and EFTA began to shift in 1973 when Denmark and the UK left EFTA to join the EEC, with Ireland. Norway, the fourth EEC applicant at the time, did not switch, following a negative national referendum. UK membership was particularly important, serving to link the three largest economies in Europe (West Germany, France and the UK) within the EEC. French President Charles de Gaulle had previously vetoed the UK's membership application—an obstacle overcome only when de Gaulle left the presidency in 1969 and compromises between the UK and the EEC were reached on the Common Agricultural Policy (CAP) and membership fees.

Importantly, the 1957 Rome Treaty included no explicit reference to environmental protection, therefore containing no explicit legal basis for community-based environmental policy (see Table 2.1). This is not particularly surprising, however. In the 1950s, the environment remained a marginal political issue everywhere in the world. Very few laws in the original member states focused on ecological issues, with the exception of mainly some conservation issues including the establishment of national parks and other protected areas. As such, there were no serious efforts by political leaders and interest groups to insert environmental provisions into a treaty focusing primarily on regional security and economic development via the expansion of free trade. The 1960s and 1970s, however, saw substantial growth in public environmental concern, proliferating scientific research (and alarm) about serious ecological and human health threats, and increasing involvement of parliaments and governments in national and international environmental management and law making.

The United Nations Conference on the Human Environment, organized in Stockholm in June 1972, proved a watershed event for both European and global environmental politics and policymaking. In many ways, this landmark meeting launched modern international

Table 2.1 List of EU treaties and key environmental provisions

Signed (in force)	Treaties and select provisions
1957 (1958)	*The Treaty of the European Economic Community* (EEC) (The Rome Treaty)
	• Established the main Community bodies and outlined their respective authorities and relationships with each other
	• Articles on the building of the single market (Art. 100), the general functioning of the Community (Art. 235), and living and working conditions in the Community (Art. 2) used to address early environmental concerns
	• Council decision rules required member state unanimity with only very limited consultation with the European Parliament
1986 (1987)	*The Single European Act (SEA)*
	• Created the European Community (EC), replacing the EEC
	• Article 100a authorized harmonization measures connected to the single market
	• Articles 130r–t recognized environmental issues as Community tasks, laying an explicit legal foundation for the adoption of environmental policy
	• Council decisions required unanimity for Articles 130r–t and introduced qualified majority voting for Article 100a (and other issues)
	• Expanded European Parliament participation in environmental policymaking through the cooperation procedure with the Council
1992 (1993)	*The Treaty on European Union* (The Maastricht Treaty)
	• Created the EU, subsuming the EC, EURATOM and the European Coal and Steel Community
	• Created the EU three-pillar system where most environmental issues fell under the first pillar
	• Council qualified majority voting was extended to most environmental policy areas
	• Made the European Parliament more equal to the Council by replacing the cooperation procedure with the co-decision procedure

Signed (in force)	Treaties and select provisions
1997 (1999)	*The Treaty of Amsterdam*
	• Addressed institutional and procedural changes to EU bodies in preparation for significant membership enlargements • Included the concept of sustainable development and strengthened commitments to environmental policy integration • Further empowered the European Parliament by expanding coverage and use of co-decision procedure to additional environmental and public health areas
2000 (2003)	*The Treaty of Nice*
	• Introduced additional changes to the main EU bodies to prepare for subsequent membership enlargements • Adjusted Council qualified majority voting to raise threshold slightly for votes needed to make a decision
2007 (2009)	*The Treaty of Lisbon*
	• Created the system of three levels of competence where environmental issues fall under shared competence • Adjusted the Council qualified majority voting system to one of double majority • Established the ordinary legislative procedure for environmental policymaking between the Council and the European Parliament

(Information compiled from treaty texts and Andrea Lenschow, "Environmental Policy: Contending Dynamics of Policy Change," in *Policy Making in the European Union*, ed. H. Wallace, W. Wallace and M. Pollack, fifth edn (Oxford: Oxford University Press, 2005), 307–30; Andrew Jordan, ed., *Environmental Policy in the European Union*, second edn (London: Earthscan, 2003))

environmental cooperation and helped make ecological issues substantially more politically important.[3] Partly a result of the Stockholm conference, countries in Europe and elsewhere began to expand political, technical and scientific cooperation around transboundary environmental issues and expand their national environmental controls and bureaucracies. Among many important international legacies of the Stockholm conference were the creation of the United Nations Environment Programme (UNEP) and the acceleration of several international environmental cooperation efforts. These included marine protection initiatives around the Baltic and Mediterranean Seas and other nascent efforts to combat European cross-border pollution—all collaborative processes in which the EEC came to play increasingly important roles as its international engagement grew tremendously from the 1970s onwards.[4]

The national leaders of the nine members met at the first summit conference of the newly enlarged EEC in Paris in September 1972.[5] Linked to the Stockholm conference, the Paris summit marks the first time EEC leaders addressed environmental issues as a group. This summit thus begins the formulation of a more collective and coherent approach to environmental policymaking and standard setting within the EEC. In retrospect, European member states leaders representing widely different political parties—including France's Georges Pompidou (Gaullist), West Germany's Willy Brandt (Social Democrat), Italy's Giulio Andreotti (Christian Democrat), and UK's Edward Heath (Conservative)—launched a political process that yielded a massive expansion of European environmental health and safety regulation and the acceleration of regional integration. Much of this was largely unforeseen at the time.

In the Paris summit declaration member state leaders formulated several basic ideas still heard in official EU environmental rhetoric and in contemporary European debates about sustainable development. Among these, the declaration stated that economic expansion was "not an end in itself" and in "the European spirit special attention will be paid to non-material values and wealth and to protection of the environment so that progress shall serve mankind."[6] This related to the Rome Treaty's goal to improve living and working conditions in all member states—treaty language quickly used by advocates as an early legal basis for greater EEC collaboration and policymaking on environmental issues alongside treaty provisions on the general functioning of the EEC and the building of the single market. The declaration requested that EEC bodies led by the European Commission work together to develop an EAP by 31 July 1973. The legacy of the Stockholm conference was thus institutionalized within the EEC.

From Paris to Brussels

Following the Paris summit, EAP development processes and the attention paid to each EAP's constituent themes played major agenda-setting roles, as the seven EAPs to date afford opportunities to identify environmental and sustainable development themes across 40-plus years, and to track varying levels of ambition in different eras (see Table 2.2). Concrete legal measures to meet EAP objectives and expand controls in identified environmental priority areas were formulated through separate policy processes which required negotiations and consensus approval by the member states in the Council of the European Union. In this era, the European Parliament was consulted on environmental issues, but lacked any real decision-making power (specific roles of major EU bodies and the ways they interact on environmental issues are discussed further in the next chapter).

The first EAP presented in 1973 boldly stated that "the aim of Community environment policy is to improve the setting and quality of life, and the surrounding and living conditions of the peoples of the Community." It introduced three basic principles for environmental action subsequently used as foundations for many EU goals and policies.[7] First, it emphasized the importance of preventive action close to the source (a precursor to the precautionary principle). Second, it stipulated that expenses of preventing and eliminating pollution should be borne by the polluter (the polluter pays principle). Third, it argued for the necessity to establish if local, national, regional or international level policy action was most appropriate, based on specific pollution types and the geographical zone in need of protection (an environmental policy version of the subsidiarity principle). The first EAP also began a process of identifying specific areas of primary concern, gradually expanded through subsequent programs. In addition, member states in 1973 established the Service for the Environment and Consumer Protection, which became a Directorate-General within the European Commission in 1982.

While the Paris summit proved important in EU environmental history, the 1970s and early 1980s was largely a reactive period. Even guided by the first three EAPs, environmental policy often evolved haphazardly, shaped by momentary political, economic and social circumstances. Environmental policymaking was also limited by the lack of any specific reference to environmental issues in the Rome Treaty. Instead, most early environment-related initiatives and policies were based on treaty provisions specifically pertaining to the operation of the single market or the broader purpose of the EEC, not environmental protection authority per se. For example, a 1967 directive on the classification, packaging and labeling of dangerous substances— long a central piece of EU chemicals law and among the earliest pieces of environmental policy—focused primarily on harmonizing national rules and standards across member states to facilitate the free exchange of goods. Not until the directive's sixth amendment in 1979 were

Table 2.2 Major components of the seven Environmental Action Programmes

First EAP (1973–76)	• Outlined basic objectives and principles guiding Community environmental policymaking
	• Focused on three categories of action: 1) reduce and prevent pollution and nuisances; 2) improve the environment and setting of life; and 3) participate in international organizations dealing with the environment
	• Concerned primarily with building scientific knowledge and methodologies and harmonizing regulatory standards across member states
Second EAP (1977–81)	• Continued many of the first EAP priorities and efforts in areas of reducing pollution and nuisances and international engagement
	• Added focus on non-damaging use and rational management of land, the environment and natural resources
	• Stressed the importance of promoting awareness of environmental problems and citizen education
Third EAP (1982–86)	• Stated that environmental policy should move beyond harmonizing divergent national standards impacting the common market and that environmental protection should be seen as a fundamental objective of the Community
	• Expanded on areas identified in the earlier EAPs, including pollution prevention and reduction; the protection and rational management of land, the environment and natural resources; and action at the international level
Fourth EAP (1987–92)	• A broader focus and more ambitious language in many areas compared to previous EAPs, consistent with greater attention to environmental issues in the SEA
	• Drew renewed attention to many issues in areas of atmospheric pollution, fresh and sea water, chemicals, biotechnology, noise, nuclear safety, management of environmental resources, and international action
	• Increased focus on the need for better implementation of existing environmental laws
Fifth EAP (1993–2000)	• Titled *Towards Sustainability* and framed in terms of the need for European and global sustainable development, heavily influenced by the Brundtland Report and member states' national plans
	• Identified five target sectors—industry, energy, transport, agriculture and tourism—around which the EU should develop goal setting and address implementation challenges
	• Stressed the importance of partnerships and consultative forums for decision making with greater involvement of industry and citizens in making and improving regulatory policy

Sixth EAP (2002–12)	• Titled *Environment 2010: Our Future, Our Choice*, it set four priority areas for urgent action: climate change; nature and biodiversity; environment and health and quality of life; and natural resources and waste
	• Outlined seven broad thematic strategies to update and expand laws on air pollution, soil protection, pesticide use, the marine environment, waste prevention and recycling, sustainable use of natural resources, and the urban environment
	• Discussed main avenues for improved action including more effective implementation and enforcement of legislation, better environmental policy integration, greater use of a blend of policy instruments, and broader public and private sector participation
Seventh EAP (2013–20)	• Titled *Living Well, Within the Limits of Our Planet*, it frames environmental policy challenges in terms of the need for more sustainable development in Europe and globally
	• Presents a long-term vision for 2050 where people live well within the planet's ecological limits, natural resources are managed sustainably, biodiversity is protected and restored, society is resilient, and low-carbon growth has long been decoupled from resource use
	• Sets three key objectives: 1) protect, conserve and enhance natural capital; 2) establish a resource-efficient, green and competitive low-carbon economy; and 3) safeguard citizens from environment-related pressures and risks to health and well-being
	• Discusses four key ways of achieving set goals: 1) improve implementation of legislation; 2) increase knowledge about the environment and widen the evidence basis for policy; 3) more and wiser investments for environment and climate policy; and 4) full integration of environmental requirements and consideration into other policy areas
	• Outlines two horizontal policy objectives: 1) make cities more sustainable; and 2) help the EU address international environmental and climate challenges more effectively

(Information compiled from the texts of the EAPs and Weale *et al., Environmental Governance in Europe*, 2000; Philip M. Hildebrand, "The European Community's Environmental Policy, 1957 to 1992: From Incidental Measures to an International Regime," *Environmental Politics* 1, no. 4 (1993): 13–44; Ecologic Institute, *Final Report for the Assessment of the 6th Environmental Action Programme* (Berlin: Ecologic Institute, 2010))

environmental concerns explicitly introduced—an amendment still largely rooted in the Rome Treaty's authority to smooth the progress of the single market.[8]

As Brussels' influence grew, the Court of Justice played a critical role in determining that environmental policy fell within the legal competence of the EEC. In a decisive 1985 ruling, expanding an earlier 1980 decision, judges stated that environmental protection was an essential EEC objective, linking to language in the Rome Treaty on improving living and working conditions across all member states.[9] In addition, by the 1980s and at the request of the European Commission, the Court of Justice had taken up several infringement procedures against member states failing to fulfill environmental policy obligations under law. Yet, legal rulings against a member state at the time resulted in little more than political embarrassment, as the European Commission had limited enforcement powers. Later treaties gave the European Commission and the Court of Justice greater authority in this area, also increasing opportunities for financial penalties on member states for non-compliance.

Landmark rulings by the Court of Justice also confirmed the close relationship between the single market and environmental policy, as the EEC attempted both to harmonize and raise national standards. Environmental leader states sometimes wanted to go beyond existing EEC policy and standards. Rulings made it clear that member states may issue domestic restrictions on environmental grounds, as long as they are non-discriminatory and proportional.[10] In the absence of EEC rules, for example, a member state may restrict the import and use of a particular product, such as a specific pesticide, to meet domestic environmental and human health standards as long as restrictions apply equally to domestic and imported products. A member state cannot regulate differently (e.g. discriminate against) chemicals coming from other member states compared to domestically produced substances. National restrictions must also be proportionate to identified environmental and human health goals, and be the least trade restrictive option for achieving the goals. The Court of Justice furthermore established that balancing environmental concerns with market interests needs to be assessed on a case-by-case basis.

The Single European Act and the environment

The 1980s saw further membership enlargement when Greece (1981), Portugal (1986), and Spain (1986) joined. Portugal thus became the third country to come from EFTA. These states' memberships were explicitly tied to domestic desires to secure transition away from authoritarian rule, starting in the 1970s, to stable democracy. They joined as relatively poor countries, hoping to stimulate their economies via foreign investment, becoming net receivers of financial support from the EEC budget (with Ireland). Member states also took important steps toward deeper cooperation and integration—after rather slow political progress in the 1960s and 1970s. A core goal of the Rome

Treaty was the creation of a single market, but by the early 1980s EEC members were far short of that goal. Thus, a major achievement of the 1986 SEA was the agreement to remove all remaining physical, fiscal and technical trade barriers by the end of 1992. Consequently, those wanting to strengthen EEC authority saw the SEA as a critical step towards greater supranationalism.

The SEA officially created the EC, replacing the EEC and incorporating EURATOM and the European Coal and Steel Community. Critically, this first amendment of the Rome Treaty established formal, legal authority for EC environmental policymaking. The SEA negotiations were not easy, revealing important differences in national interests and preferences among the 12 member states. A few northern member states, most notably Denmark, Germany and the Netherlands, wanted a single market with comparatively high environmental protection standards. In contrast, southern member states such as Greece, Italy, Portugal and Spain focused more on traditional economic development, desiring a single market with more limited environmental protection standards. Contentious SEA negotiations resulted in several compromises between these two groups. Northern member states got a single market with clear legal provisions for adopting environmental laws, while the southern member states got the creation of EC structural funds with economic resources for domestic development projects in support of economic and social cohesion.[11]

The SEA was a watershed moment for European environmental politics and policymaking. Environmental laws could now be passed under one of two sets of treaty articles. Article 100a authorized the adoption of additional harmonization measures to expand the operation of the single market, generally formalizing and further institutionalizing existing practices and policies. Articles 130r, 130s and 130t focused explicitly on the need for environmental protection measures. Whether a specific issue was decided under Article 100a or Articles 130r–t had important implications for decision making among member states in the Council of the European Union. Decisions under Articles 130r–t still had to be taken unanimously by all member states, whereas Article 100a for the first time required only a qualified majority. In subsequent treaty reforms, majority decision making was expanded to almost all environmental issues, with only a few remaining exceptions: environmental measures with fiscal implications, energy supply issues, land use, town and country planning, and quantitative management of water resources (see Table 2.1).

One of the SEA's most important institutional changes for law making was the introduction of the so-called cooperation procedure on environmental issues, under which member states took decisions through qualified majority voting (e.g. under Article 100a). The cooperation procedure gave the European Parliament a greater, if still limited, role in environmental policy adoption. Now the European Parliament was given the right, during a first reading, to issue an opinion on a new legislative proposal issued by the European Commission. The Council of the European Union would then adopt a common position through qualified majority on the proposal, which the European Parliament could amend or reject during a second reading. However, member states retained final decision-making power, as they were free to ignore the European Parliament's position if a bill amended or rejected by the European Parliament during its second reading was passed unanimously in the Council of the European Union.

The SEA changes providing a clearer legal basis for decision making and strengthening EU bodies ushered in a substantial expansion of environmental policies, some enacted under the environmental provisions and others (as before) under the single market authority. In practice, the breadth of the new environmental provisions alongside those on the single market meant that many associated issues could fall under EC authority, as long as the European Commission and most member states were willing to take them on—with the European Parliament clamoring for more influence and looking to expand its participation beyond the cooperation procedure. As the central role of Brussels in European environmental politics was cemented, the late 1980s marks the beginning of one of the most expansive periods of EC environmental law making. The two post-SEA EAPs—the fourth and the fifth—also demonstrate the leaps forward in environmental policy focus, using much more ambitious language in expressing policy goals, highlighting additional priorities for action, and calling attention to problems with environmental policy implementation.

Maastricht and the EU

Building on the SEA and fuelled by optimism surrounding the Cold War's end and German reunification, European institution building accelerated rapidly in the 1990s. The 1992 Treaty on European Union (commonly called the Maastricht Treaty after the Dutch city where it was adopted) officially created the EU, subsuming the EC. This second amendment of the Rome Treaty was another significant victory for those wanting a stronger and more supranational EC. Through the creation of an official Union, it greatly deepened European political and economic integration, including a timetable for creating a monetary union, leading to the introduction of an electronic euro in January 1999 and the transition to everyday use of the euro currency in most (but not all) member states in January of 2002. The Maastricht Treaty expanded the scope of EU authority, introduced legal provisions for the Court of Justice to impose financial penalties on member states that failed to fulfill their obligations correctly under EU law, and stipulated that the promotion of sustainable growth respecting the environment was a principal EU objective.

Importantly, the Maastricht Treaty divided the EU into three main policy areas (or "pillars"). Within each pillar were different balances between supranational and intergovernmental principles and decision making. Supranationalism was strongest in the first pillar, involving joint decision making by the European Commission, the Council of the European Union, and the European Parliament. It included political and economic issues previously covered by the EC (as well as EURATOM and the European Coal and Steel Community), including the customs union, the single market, competition law, and the CAP and the Common Fisheries Policy (CFP). Most environment-related issues also fell under the first pillar, placing them firmly within the EU's most supranational remit. In the second pillar, the Common Foreign and Security Policy, member states maintained most decision-making authority on matters such as peacekeeping, human rights and foreign aid. The third pillar included Police and Judicial Cooperation in Criminal Matters, where member states also retained sovereign rights over national decisions, with inter-state cooperation focused on issues such as terrorism, drug trafficking, weapons smuggling, human trafficking, and organized crime.

The Maastricht Treaty established a legal basis for the EAPs (earlier programs were merely political documents issued by the European Commission). Since Maastricht, EAPs are prepared by the European Commission and adopted by the European Parliament and the Council of the European Union, having the status of formal legal acts. As with the SEA, many of the Maastricht Treaty's most important ramifications for environmental politics and policymaking were procedural. Perhaps chief among these was the introduction of the co-decision procedure, replacing the cooperation procedure for 15 areas ("legal bases") which included several covering the single market and related environmental issues.[12] This major step toward putting the European Parliament on more equal footing with the Council of the European Union on environmental policymaking, where member states used qualified majority voting for a greater number of issues, outlined a complex series of deliberations in each of the two bodies. As a result, they largely shared authority and responsibility to pass new environmental laws. Since then, the views of the Members of the European Parliament (MEPs) had to be included during final decision making.

Expanding the European Parliament's authority and areas subject to member state majority voting worked, in practice, to facilitate EU environmental policy expansion—often via green member state leadership and political pressure from within the European Commission and the European Parliament. The fifth EAP pushed the EU to engage more actively international environmental and sustainable development goals, as the 1990s saw more aggressive policymaking in many environmental and public health areas. In addition, the end of the Cold War opened opportunities for three more countries to join the EU in 1995: Austria, Finland and Sweden. They previously eschewed membership for a variety of reasons related to their military neutrality and proximity to the Soviet Bloc. As European security concerns changed radically in the early 1990s, Austria, Finland and Sweden saw greater political and economic benefits of integration within the single market, further shrinking EFTA membership. During the same era, Norwegian voters rejected EU membership for a second time.

The addition of Austria, Finland, and Sweden impacted EU environmental politics and policymaking in multiple ways. They joined as relatively wealthy countries, immediately becoming reliable net contributors to the EU budget, including funds for environment and development projects in member states and applicant countries. All three new members also had generally high environmental standards. In fact, membership negotiations involved their efforts to retain some domestic regulations that were more stringent than those in the EU. Upon membership, their interests often led them to join Germany, Denmark and the Netherlands in pushing for higher pan-European environmental standards—with the UK also taking an increased leadership role on environmental issues in the 1990s. The same applies for many of these countries' MEPs. As such, their involvement with the European Commission, the Council of the European Union, and the European Parliament shaped much EU environmental law making in the late 1990s and early 2000s.

EU membership for Austria, Finland and Sweden substantially changed the EU-EFTA relationship, which was also reshaped by the 1992 European Economic Area treaty (coming into effect in 1994). This treaty formally linked the three EFTA members Iceland, Liechtenstein and Norway with the EU. It incorporated these countries into the single market and established that EU environmental (and other) laws related to the operation of the single market should apply to them. Importantly, the treaty does not cover the CAP or CFP, the customs union, or the common trade policy. The fourth remaining EFTA country, Switzerland, was part of the treaty negotiations but the agreement was rejected by Swiss voters in a 1992 national referendum. This effectively halted Switzerland's EU membership application, submitted earlier that year. Instead, Switzerland's relationship with the EU and the single market is outlined in a series of bilateral agreements containing provisions on harmonization with EU environmental policies similar to those in the European Economic Area treaty.

The application of the European Economic Area treaty greatly favors the EU because of the three EFTA countries' substantial interest in having access to the single market. There is a "safety valve" in that the Joint Committee consisting of representatives of all EU and EFTA countries plus the European External Action Service (EEAS)—the EU's diplomatic arm in its external relations—requires unanimity to add an act to the treaty based on new EU legislation.[13] However, EFTA countries' bargaining position is weak, given their fear of the political and economic consequences of rejecting an EU law. Thus, the Europeanization of EFTA countries is characterized by a deep conflict between diplomacy and democracy. In this respect, one observer described Norway as a "fax democracy"—EU legislation, including environmental laws, arrives in a steady stream of faxes from Brussels to Oslo for incorporation into Norwegian law without much national parliamentary or public debate or ability to influence incoming decisions and standards.[14] Nevertheless, the European Economic Area treaty and the bilateral agreements with Switzerland make clear that many EU environmental provisions extend to the EFTA members.

From Amsterdam to Lisbon and beyond

The 1997 Amsterdam Treaty and the 2000 Nice Treaty continued the period of relatively rapid integration, making changes to the composition and operation of EU bodies to accommodate major enlargements and deepening cooperation. Areas of member state qualified majority voting were further expanded to the point where only a few—including taxation, social security, foreign policy, defense, and police cooperation—still require unanimity. The European Parliament once again gained greater authority through further expansions of the co-decision procedure, putting it on par with the Council of the European Union on much decision making, including on most environmental issues. Although the positions of environmental policy integration and sustainable development were solidified within the EU, the Amsterdam and Nice treaties contained fewer environmental policy-related modifications than previous treaty amendments. Instead, their main impacts were in facilitating the entrance of a large number of Central, Eastern and Southern European countries. In 2004, 10 countries joined: Cyprus, Czech Republic, Estonia, Hungary, Latvia, Lithuania, Malta, Poland, Slovakia and Slovenia. Bulgaria and Romania became members in 2007.

In general, environmental issues played a relatively small part in the membership processes leading to the 2004 and 2007 enlargements, but the impact on the new members was substantial. All new member states were required to accept the full body of EU environmental law before accession, establish new agencies and reorganize old ones, and embark on implementation and enforcement processes. Many of the massive environmental policy changes across the new members seen prior to enlargement would not have been achieved without regulatory pressure and funding from the EU. While many EU environmental activists, analysts and policymakers feared that the inclusion of so many new and relatively poor member states would greatly slow or substantially weaken EU environmental policymaking, such dire predictions proved largely erroneous—environmental policy was too institutionalized as a central first pillar issue.[15] Furthermore, the new member states have not typically acted as a bloc, illustrating that they often have their own individual interests and priorities (just like the older member states).

In the wake of the adoption of multiple EU treaties between 1986 and 2000, European political leaders negotiated a new European constitution to solidify all legal mandates into a single document. While the constitution was approved early on in a few member states, it was rejected by national referendums in influential countries—including France and the Netherlands—in the summer of 2005, effectively halting the constitutional process. Instead, member state governments settled for negotiating and adopting the 2007 Lisbon Treaty, entering into force in 2009. Whereas the constitution would have replaced all earlier treaties, from Rome to Nice, the Lisbon Treaty merely modifies existing agreements (like the treaties before it). The description of roles, authorities and relationships of the major EU bodies, discussed in the next chapter, reflects the current situation in the EU, following the entry into force of the Lisbon Treaty and 2013 Croatian membership. The Lisbon Treaty also made the EU a formal legal entity, meaning that it can enter into contracts and join international conventions and international organizations (previously, that right had officially belonged to the EC).

The Lisbon Treaty introduced a number of important institutional changes. Among these, it abolished the three pillar structure in place since 1992, instead distinguishing between three main categories or levels of competencies across all policy fields where the EU is involved. First are areas where the EU has exclusive competence and legislates alone. This covers issues such as the customs union, competition rules, monetary policy for euro countries, and the common trade policy. Second are areas of shared competence where the EU and member states make decisions jointly, covering the single market, social policy, environmental policy, consumer protection, transport, and energy. In the third category, member states have exclusive competence in decision making but the EU can provide supporting competence. These areas include education, health care, culture, tourism, and civil protection. In addition, the Lisbon Treaty includes the Charter of Fundamental Rights and, for the first time, a clause about withdrawal from the EU. Earlier treaties contained no provisions for exit.

The Lisbon Treaty continued to expand the co-decision procedure, now officially called the ordinary legislative procedure. From the 15 areas of co-decision introduced in the Maastricht Treaty, the list was expanded to 44 areas by the Nice Treaty. The Lisbon Treaty nearly doubled the scope of co-decision, so that the ordinary legislative procedure now covers 85 areas. There was a steady increase in the number of legal files adopted by co-decision during sessions of the European Parliament: 165 files in 1993–99; 403 files in 1999–2004; and 447 files in 2004–09.[16] Most were non-environmental, but environmental issues (including the CAP and the CFP), energy, consumer safety and public health protection are critical areas of co-decision, as a total of 650 files were finalized under the ordinary legislative procedure during the 2009–14 legislative period.[17] Still, some politically sensitive issues remain under the special legislative procedure where member states closely guard their sovereignty and the European Parliament still lacks equality with the Council of the European Union, including foreign policy.

EU bodies and member states continue to pay substantial attention to environmental issues, a major policy area of shared competence and collective decision making. The sixth EAP paid greater attention to climate change than earlier EAPs, and continued to focus on biodiversity, natural resources, waste, and health and quality of life, as all of these issues were framed in the discourse of sustainability. However, it was not clear that there would be a seventh EAP, given the reluctance of some in the European Commission and a few member states to set ambitious goals for additional environmental policy development.

Nevertheless, the seventh EAP carries on the language of sustainability, presenting a long-term vision for 2050 where societies have learned to live within planetary boundaries. To this end, the program establishes another set of key objectives for the time period up to 2020. It notes that inadequate implementation and enforcement of EU environmental legislation as well as a lack of policy coherence across issue areas remain important factors preventing the EU and member states from meeting critical objectives.

Sustainable development, economic growth and policy integration

While interrelated environment and development debates go back at least to the 1972 Stockholm conference and scholarship in the 1970s, the EU began to explicitly engage the concept of sustainable development—integrating ecological concerns with social progress and economic growth—more explicitly in the 1980s. As a sign of the concept's growing importance in Europe, the fifth EAP adopted in 1992—the same year the United Nations Conference on Environment and Development (also known as the "Earth Summit") was organized in Rio de Janeiro, Brazil—was entitled *Towards Sustainability*. This EAP shaped the EU's legislative agenda for much of the 1990s around sustainable development. It built on national environmental plans, with their roots in the 1987 Brundtland Report, *Our Common Future*, framing sustainable development at multiple levels from global to local and attempting to avoid long-term ecological damage while recognizing the need for socially progressive development.[18]

The Maastricht Treaty referenced sustainability and the Amsterdam Treaty made sustainable development an overall EU objective. Building on this legal commitment, in 2001 the European Council adopted the first EU-wide Sustainable Development Strategy, based on an earlier European Council request that the European Commission prepare "a proposal for a long-term strategy dovetailing policies for economically, socially and ecologically sustainable development." The sixth EAP was intended to provide the environmental component of the 2001 Sustainable Development Strategy. Like the Amsterdam Treaty, the Sustainable Development Strategy identifies sustainable development as a key principle to govern all EU internal policies and activities and guide its external relations with other countries and multilateral forums. In 2006 the European Council adopted a revised Sustainable Development Strategy, following the addition of 10 new members in 2004 (and in anticipation of two more in 2007), but without altering any fundamental commitments or perspectives on sustainability.

The 2006 Sustainable Development Strategy describes a host of goals and needed actions on climate and energy, transport, consumption and production, public health, social inclusion/demography/migration, and global poverty and sustainable development. Within a context increasingly dominated by ecological modernization in Europe, the strategy and the EAPs embrace a "weak" version of sustainability. They focus on win-win solutions involving positive gains from technological development and enhanced economic efficiency, where societal transitions provide opportunities for new products and markets fuelling continued economic growth. Despite a strong legal and rhetorical commitment, European Commission reviews and progress reports on the implementation of the Sustainable Development Strategy in 2007 and 2009 concluded that while some progress is noted, most important policy objectives were not translated into substantial and concrete action and many unsustainable trends continued across Europe.[19] Nevertheless, in late 2009 member states leaders reiterated that "sustainable development remains a fundamental objective of the European Union under the Lisbon treaty."[20]

The EU Sustainable Development Strategy developed alongside efforts to strengthen European economic competitiveness. Enthusiastically endorsed by EU bodies and political leaders in member states, the so-called Lisbon Strategy on competitiveness was adopted in 2000, outlining a 10-year program to make the EU "the most competitive and dynamic knowledge-based economy in the world, capable of sustainable economic growth with more and better jobs and greater social cohesion." The Lisbon Strategy's agenda focused on creating jobs and stimulating economic growth, formulated in response to fears of many European politicians that Europe was falling behind North America and Asia in innovation and competitiveness, as economic globalization and trade liberalization increased competition among countries and firms.[21] Thus, the Lisbon Strategy underlined the EU's focus on continued economic growth as a basis for maintaining the social welfare state in Europe.

The Lisbon Strategy's 10-year program was replaced by the Europe 2020 Strategy adopted in 2010. Reflecting how ecological modernization has come close to being an official ideology of the EU, the Europe 2020 Strategy identifies three key drivers for growth to be implemented through concrete actions at EU and national levels: 1) smart growth (fostering knowledge, innovation, education, and a digital society); 2) sustainable growth (making production more resource efficient while boosting competitiveness); and 3) inclusive growth (raising participation in the labor market, the acquisition of skills and the fight against poverty). Critics argue, however, that expecting economic growth and markets to produce sustainability is incompatible with a deeper inter-generational commitment to live within local, national, regional and global ecological limits.[22] The outcomes of the Lisbon Strategy partially support this skepticism, given that its advocates tend to cite the pro-business reforms and technological and research investments made as its greatest achievements, with little suggestion that Europe was made more ecologically sustainable via the 10-year effort.[23]

Even though EU leaders and the European Commissions have repeatedly stressed the existence of synergies and complementarities between the Sustainable Development Strategy and the Lisbon Strategy/ Europe 2020 Strategy, critical relationships between the implementation of the two sets of initiatives remain unclear.[24] This highlights the importance—and difficulty—of environmental policy integration.[25] Environmental concerns must be better incorporated into transport, energy, trade, fiscal policy, corporate governance, agriculture and so on if key objectives are to be achieved. For example, if environmental goals include lowering GHG emissions while transport and housing policies facilitate ever more suburban, car-dependent sprawl and high-way construction as fewer resources are invested in public transportation—currently a common combination in many European countries—then these policy areas are not well integrated toward achieving greater sustainability. While environmental policy integration is discussed in several of the later EAPs and a host of EU documents, it remains very difficult to accomplish at deeper institutional levels.

Notes

1 Albert Weale, "Environmental Rules and Rule-making in the European Union," *Journal of European Public Policy* 3, no. 4 (1996): 594–611; Albert Weale *et al., Environmental Governance in Europe: An Ever Closer Ecological Union?* (Oxford: Oxford University Press, 2000).

2 Institute for European Environmental Policy, *Sourcebook on EU Environmental Law* (Brussels: Institute for European Environmental Policy, 2010).

3 Björn-Ola Linnér and Henrik Selin, "The Road to Rio: Early Efforts on Environment and Development," in *Global Challenges: Furthering the Multilateral Process for Sustainable Development*, ed. A. Churie Kallhauge, G. Sjöstedt and E. Corell (London: Greenleaf Publishing, 2005), 58–73.

4 Stacy D. VanDeveer, "Assessment Information in European Politics: East and West," in *Global Environmental Assessments: Information and Influence*, ed. R. Mitchell, W. Clark, D. Cash and N. Dickson (Cambridge, Mass.: MIT Press, 2006).

5 John McCormick, *Environmental Policy in the European Union* (New York: Palgrave, 2001).

6 The First Summit Conference of the Enlarged Community, E.C. Bull, no. 10 (1972).
7 Philip M. Hildebrand, "The European Community's Environmental Policy, 1957 to 1992: From Incidental Measures to an International Regime," *Environmental Politics* 1, no. 4 (1993): 13–44.
8 Henrik Selin, "Coalition Politics and Chemicals Management in a Regulatory Ambitious Europe," *Global Environmental Politics* 7, no. 3 (2007): 63–93.
9 Ludwig Krämer, "The European Court of Justice," in *Environmental Policy in the EU: Actors, Institutions and Processes*, ed. Andrew Jordan and Camilla Adelle, third edn (London: Earthscan, 2012), 113–31.
10 Henrik Selin and Stacy D. VanDeveer, "Politics of Trade and Environment in the European Union," in *Handbook on Trade and Environment*, ed. K.P. Gallagher (Aldershot: Edward Elgar, 2008), 194–203.
11 Weale *et al., Environmental Governance in Europe*, 57.
12 The Maastricht Treaty does not actually contain the word "co-decision" to describe this policymaking process, but it quickly became the commonly used description by EU bodies, member states and analysts.
13 The European Commission used to represent the EU in the Joint Commission, but the Lisbon Treaty transferred this authority to the EEAS, officially launched in 2011—the EU's "diplomatic corps" supporting the high representative of the Union for foreign affairs and security policy.
14 Eivind Hovden, "Norway: Top Down Europeanization by Fax," in *Environmental Policy in Europe: The Europeanization of National Environmental Policy*, ed. Andrew Jordan and Duncan Liefferink (New York: Routledge, 2005), 154–71.
15 JoAnn Carmin and Stacy D. VanDeveer, *EU Enlargement and the Environment* (London: Routledge, 2005).
16 European Parliament, *Codecision and Conciliation: A Guide to how the Parliament Co-Legislates under the Treaty of Lisbon* (2012).
17 European Parliament, *Directorate for Plenary Sessions, Legislative Procedures Voted in Plenary 7th Parliamentary Term 2009–14* (2014).
18 World Commission on Environment and Development, *Our Common Future* (Oxford: Oxford University Press, 1987).
19 European Commission, *Communication from the Commission to the European Parliament, the Council, the European Economic and Social Committee and the Committee of the Regions—Mainstreaming Sustainable Development into EU Policies: 2009 Review of the European Union Strategy for Sustainable Development, COM* (2009), 0400 final (2009).
20 European Council, *Conclusions*, Article 21 (December 2009), www.con silium.europa.eu/uedocs/cms_data/docs/pressdata/en/ec/111877.pdf.
21 Maria João Rodrigues, ed., *Europe, Globalization and the Lisbon Agenda* (Cheltenham: Edward Elgar, 2009).
22 Paul Wapner, *Living through the End of Nature* (Cambridge, Mass.: MIT Press, 2010); John Barry, *The Politics of Actually Existing Sustainability* (Oxford: Oxford University Press, 2012).
23 Rodrigues, *Europe, Globalization and the Lisbon Agenda*.
24 Marc Pallemaerts, "Developing More Sustainably?" in *Environmental Policy in the EU: Actors, Institutions and Processes*, ed. Andrew Jordan and Camilla Adelle, third edn (New York: Earthscan, 2013).

25 Andrea Lenschow, ed., *Environmental Policy Integration: Greening Sectoral Policies in Europe* (London: Earthscan, 2002); William Lafferty and Eivind Hovden, "Environmental Policy Integration: Towards an Analytical Framework," *Environmental Politics* 12, no. 3 (2003): 1–22; Andrew J. Jordan and Andrea Lenschow, eds, *Innovation in Environmental Policy? Integrating the Environment for Sustainability* (Northampton, Mass.: Edward Elgar, 2008).

3 EU actors and policy instruments

- **Main EU bodies in environmental governance**
- **Lobby groups and civil society**
- **EU environmental policy instruments**
- **EU budgets and the environment**

As a highly complex governance system, the EU lacks a clearly defined organizational center. In fact, it has been characterized as a "relatively *leaderless* system of governance."[1] Authority and influence are dispersed across several bodies established and substantially reformed over time via the series of foundational treaties negotiated, signed, and ratified by member states.[2] Following the Lisbon Treaty, seven official bodies constitute the organizational core of the EU:

1 the European Council;
2 the European Commission;
3 the Council of the European Union;
4 the European Parliament;
5 the Court of Justice;
6 the Court of Auditors; and
7 the European Central Bank.

In addition, a large number of other EU bodies fulfill various political and/or functional roles. These bodies, to varying degrees, also interact with a multitude of non-state actors attempting to shape decisions and protect their interests and rights. Like the member states, EU bodies and the non-state organizations are impacted in multiple ways by a growing number of EU policies and programs.

This chapter analyzes the main EU actors in environmental governance and their use of different environmental policy instruments. It begins by examining the main functions of the five official EU bodies most active in environmental governance—the European Council, the European Commission, the Council of the European Union, the European Parliament, and the Court of Justice—as well as related activities of other bodies including advisory committees and specialized agencies. Next, the roles of lobby groups and civil society in EU environmental politics are discussed, followed by a section examining the use of different categories of policy instruments within the growing body of EU environmental law. The chapter ends with a brief overview of the EU budget with a particular focus on how different budget items relate to environmental issues and governance. This chapter thereby lays the groundwork for Chapter 4, paying more detailed attention to the roles of EU bodies, member states, stakeholder groups and civil society in the formulation, implementation, and enforcement of environmental policy, and Chapter 5, discussing policy developments in discrete environmental issue areas.

Main EU bodies in environmental governance

The European Council is the highest-level forum for discussion and negotiation between political leaders of member states and EU bodies. It began meeting informally in 1974, acquired formal status in 1992, and became an official EU body in 2009 via the Lisbon Treaty. Initially, European Council meetings brought together member state heads of state or government and the president of the European Commission. The Lisbon Treaty created two new permanent positions chosen by the European Council, aiming to provide more stable representation for the EU internationally: the President of the European Council (serving a two and half term, renewable once) and the High Representative of the Union for Foreign Affairs and Security Policy (selected for a five year term). The President of the European Council, currently Donald Tusk, previously Prime Minister of Poland and first elected in 2014, chairs European Council meetings and is a principal spokenperson of the EU on the world stage. (This is not the equivalent to a "President" of the EU.) The High Representative of the Union for Foreign Affairs and Security Policy, since 2014 the former Italian Foreign Minister Federica Mogherini, coordinates the Common Foreign and Security Policy with support from EEAS. The person holding this position partecipates in European Council debates on foreign policy and security issues, and serves as Vice-President in the European Commission.

Each member state holds the Presidency of the European Council for six months, on a rotating basis. The European Council meets at least twice every six months, serving two major purposes: setting the

EU's general political direction and identifying future political priorities, and dealing with controversial issues that cannot be resolved at lower intergovernmental levels or under existing EU law. Thus, while the European Council has no formal law-making authority, it serves influential agenda-setting and problem-solving functions. No major political developments happen without the approval of member state leaders, including the adoption of new treaties or other major institutional reform proposals. Sometimes the European Council is also directly involved in environment and sustainable development initiatives. For example, the European Council played important roles in negotiating and revising the EU's Sustainable Development Strategy and reaching member state agreement around the EU's internal and international climate change and energy goals.[3]

The European Commission was established through the Rome Treaty and is tasked to drive deeper integration and sustainable development. Over the years, the European Commission experienced substantial organizational changes as it grew into a large body, employing almost 33,000 people in 2013.[4] The majority of staff is stationed in Brussels, but the European Commission maintains offices in all member states and 130 locations around the world. Everyone employed by the European Commission represents the EU, rather than the national interest of their home countries. EU treaties give the European Commission several legal and political roles, including: 1) exclusive power to propose new EU legislation, meaning that all policy proposals originate from within the European Commission; 2) monitor implementation of EU law in member states; 3) take enforcement action when member states fail to meet their obligations under EU law; 4) manage the EU budget; and 5) represent the EU internationally alongside other official delegates and member state representatives. These rights and capacities make the European Commission a central actor in EU environmental governance and a major force in international environmental and trade cooperation.

The European Commission is led by a President who is elected for a five-year term (renewal possible) by a simple majority in the European Parliament, following a proposal by the European Council. The President, who for the 2014–19 period is the former Prime Minister of Luxembourg, Jean-Claude Juncker, presides over the College of Commissioners (each member also serving five-year, renewable terms). The expansion of member states starting in the 1970s resulted in a growing number of Commissioners: the 2009–14 European Commission following Croatia's accession consisted of one President and 27 Commissioners. To streamline the bureaucracy, the Lisbon Treaty stipulates that starting in 2014 only two-thirds of member states should have a Commissioner, based on a revolving system. Member states, however, took a unanimous decision to continue the system of having the President or one Commissioner from each member state. The president-elect selects Commissioners in consultation with member state governments and assigns them areas of responsibilities (holding the right to decide how the European Commission is organizationally structured and which portfolio is assigned to which Commissioner). The new European Commission must be collectively approved by the European Parliament before beginning work. Once in office, the President and Commissioners cannot be removed by national governments.

Under the President, there is currently one First Vice President, the High Representative of the Union for Foreign Affairs and Security Policy, and five Vice Presidents who manage broader cross-cutting issue areas (such as "the Energy Union"). The First Vice President coordinate the work of the other 20 Commissioners in charge of the issue-specific portfolios, supported by departments called Directorates-General (DGs) that are headed by a Director General. One Commissioner is in charge of the Environment, Maritime Affairs and Fisheries portfolio that includes DG Environment and DG Maritime Affairs and Fisheries (previously, these two DGs were lead by separate Commissioners). Other Commissioners respectively manage the Climate Action and Energy portfolio (involving DG Climate Action and DG Energy, which earlier also operated under two different Commissioners), the Agriculture and Rural Development portfolio (handled by DG Agriculture and Rural Development), and the Health and Food Safety portfolio (where DG Health and Consumers plays a central role). From modest origins, DG Environment has emerged as one of the more important DGs, frequently expanding and shaping new policies. The EU's goal of integrating environmental concerns into other policy areas has also facilitates a growth in DG Environment's influence, but the record of engendering such policy integration domestically within member states remains mixed.[5]

The Council of the European Union (previously called the Council of Ministers) was established in the Rome Treaty and consists of member state government representatives. Its work is supported by a Secretariat staff of approximately 3,500 people.[6] Meetings often take place in Brussels, but ministers can gather in other places. During meetings, member states negotiate based on their national interests as they seek to develop common positions. The Council of the European Union is divided into nine topical areas. The Environment Council deals with all environmental issues (including climate change). Agricultural and fishery-related issues are sent to the Agriculture and Fisheries Council. The Council of the European Union passes EU environmental law, together with the European Parliament, under the ordinary legislative procedure. It also has the authority to sign international environmental agreements on behalf of the EU.

The Lisbon Treaty establishes the current voting system. From 1 November 2014, it takes a qualified majority of 55 percent of member states (16 of 28), representing at least 65 percent of the EU's population, for a proposal to pass. This is sometimes referred to as "double majority." To make it more difficult for a small number of the most populous member states to prevent a decision, a blocking minority must comprise at least four member states; otherwise, the necessary majority is deemed reached even if the population criterion is not met. However, until 2017 a member state may request that decisions are taken in accordance with the previous qualified majority system. To pass a decision under this old system, two conditions have to be met. First, the proposal must be supported by 255 out of 345 votes (73.91 percent). Four countries—Germany, France, Italy and UK—each have 29 votes, while other countries have a smaller number of votes, down to Luxembourg with four and Malta with three. Second, the proposal must be backed by a majority of member states (15 out of 28). In addition, a member state may request verification that the member states which constituted a qualified majority represent at least 62 percent of the total EU population.

The European Parliament dates back to the Rome Treaty, referring to the Common Assembly which was renamed the European Parliament in 1962. MEPs were initially part-time delegates from member states' national parliaments, but have been full-time delegates selected through direct national elections every five years since 1979 (each new European Commission is selected the same year).[7] With enlargements, the size of the European Parliament gradually increased up to 766 seats following Croatia's membership, but starting with the 2014–19 European Parliament the size is capped to 751 MEPs—750 voting MEPs plus the non-voting president of the Parliament. Seats are distributed among member states relative to national population, but not according to the same ratio as smaller countries are somewhat over-represented to curb the influence of the largest member states. Germany is the only country to have the maximum number of MEPs (96), followed by France (74 seats), Italy and the UK (73 seats), and descending down to a minimum of six seats (Cyprus, Estonia, Luxembourg and Malta). MEPs sit in multinational political groups, rather than national blocs. The work of the European Parliament is divided between Strasbourg (plenary sessions), Brussels (committee meetings), and Luxembourg (staff offices).

The European Parliament passes environmental law under the ordinary legislative procedure in conjunction with the Council of the European Union. As in national parliaments, much legislative work is carried out in issue-specific standing committees, one of which is the Environment, Public Health and Food Safety Committee. Each committee has a chairperson, three vice-chairpersons, and various committee members. Reports on particular policy proposals are usually compiled by a rapporteur who is appointed by the chairperson of the committee, selected from among committee members. The influence of the Environment, Public Health and Food Safety Committee, and the European Parliament as a whole, has greatly increased over environmental policymaking since the SEA. While MEPs have frequently succeeded in adding "green" amendments to proposed policies, recent years have seen some shift toward more modest environmental influence.[8] The European Parliament in committees and plenary (at different stages in the environmental law-making process) makes decisions either by simple majority (a majority of members voting), or absolute majority (a majority of all members: 376 out of 751 MEPs).

The Court of Justice, established under the Rome Treaty, is located in Luxembourg. It consists of one judge from each member state and eight advocates-general who serve six-year renewable terms. For the sake of efficiency when hearing cases, the Court of Justice rarely gathers in full, but usually sits in chambers of 13, five, or three judges. The judges seek uniform interpretation and application of the EU treaties. The advocates-general are tasked with presenting reasoned opinions, seeking impartiality in all cases. Five of the eight advocates-general are always nominated by the five largest member states (Germany, France, the United Kingdom, Italy, and Spain), while the other three rotate in alphabetical order of other member states. To cope with a growing case load and offer individuals better legal protection, a lower-level General Court was established in 1989 to rule on certain cases, including actions brought by individuals and companies against EU acts and bodies, as well as actions by member states against the European Commission or the Council of the European Union.

Proceedings in front of the Court of Justice may be contentious or non-contentious. Contentious proceedings can be initiated by an EU body, member state, or private person. These include proceedings where the Court of Justice rules on conflicts between member states, between EU bodies, between the European Commission and a member state, or between private persons and EU bodies. Non-contentious proceedings denote cooperation between the Court of Justice and national courts within member states. National courts can voluntarily ask the Court of Justice for a preliminary ruling when they apply EU law domestically. Such rulings are binding on national courts; if they ask for advice, they must follow it as they consider domestic cases. With greater EU authority and more environmental policy, the influence of the Court of Justice on policymaking, implementation and member state law has increased sharply. Since the 1970s, the Court of Justice has issued over 700 judgments related to environmental matters, most initiated by the European Commission against a member state, substantially shaping EU environmental law and implementation in the process.[9]

Box 3.1 Two other official EU bodies

The *Court of Auditors*, in Luxembourg, may audit any person or organization (including member states) handling EU funds. It presents the European Parliament and the Council with an annual report on the previous financial year, and findings related to specific cases, including environmental projects, are summarized in reports submitted to the European Commission and national governments. If auditors discover fraud or irregularities, they inform the European Anti-Fraud Office.

The *European Central Bank* (ECB), in Frankfurt, collaborates with the member state central banks with a focus on keeping prices and financial systems stable. The ECB leads the cooperation between central banks in the euro zone (i.e. countries using the euro as their currency). It is not directly involved in environmental affairs, but the overall strength of the European economy has impacts on the formulation of environmental goals and policy.

Beyond the official bodies, the Committee of the Regions and the European Economic and Social Committee have formal, treaty-based advisory roles and must be consulted by the European Commission, the Council of the European Union and the European Parliament. Both committees have 353 members assigned proportionally from member states based on their total population. The Committee of Regions, established by the Maastricht Treaty and made up of elected members of local and regional authorities, formulates opinions on a host of policy issues, including environmental ones. This directly brings perspectives of sub-national jurisdictions, which are responsible for implementing much of EU law, into EU policymaking processes as well as acts as a link between the EU and citizens. The European Economic and Social Committee, which originates in the Rome Treaty and consists of representatives of employer and worker organizations and other organized interests such as farmers and consumer groups, issues opinions on socioeconomic issues including the single market, many of which intersect with energy and environmental policymaking. Yet, the direct influence of the two consultative committees, having "voice, but no vote," is limited.[10]

Member states, in collaboration with the European Commission and the European Parliament, also have created a growing number of specialized agencies within discrete policy areas through separate legal acts (e.g. they are not treaty-based bodies).[11] By 2014, over 40 such agencies were in operation. One is the European Institute of Innovation and Technology, seeking to pool education, scientific and business resources in support of the development of new technologies benefiting European industry. Two agencies support activities under the EURATOM treaty. Several "executive agencies" operate for a fixed time period as they help the European Commission to manage individual EU programs in areas such as education, culture, research and public health. The majority of specialized agencies, however, are "decentralized agencies." These permanent organizations are located all over Europe (where the initial placing of a specific agency can involve much competition among member states seeking to attract the prestige, jobs and other benefits that come with hosting it).

The increase in agencies reflects the growing scope of the EU agenda and the functional need for new bodies to enhance the strength and uniformity of regulation, but many political interests of the European Commission, the European Parliament and member states over regulatory authority go into their design, effectively expanding the "Eurocracy."[12] Some analysts portray the agencies as dominated by national governments reluctant to cede much sovereignty. Other studies afford the agencies greater independence even as they operate closely with relevant European Commission DGs, related committees within the Council of the European Union and the European Parliament, and national regulatory bodies.[13] The agencies, which typically have rather modest formal mandates to deal with administrative and informational issues, may in their day-to-day operations exercise overt influence over important regulatory issues. Thus, their activities can have far-reaching political consequences, shaping a broad range of policy decisions by the European Commission, the European Parliament and member states.

Primarily four decentralized agencies address environmental issues. The European Environment Agency (EEA), located in Copenhagen, was established in 1990 and began operating in 1994. The EEA has 33 official members (the EU-28, plus Iceland, Lichtenstein, Norway, Switzerland, and Turkey), and five cooperating countries (Macedonia, Albania, Bosnia and Herzegovina, Montenegro, and Serbia). The EEA lacks overt regulatory authority. Rather, it gathers and assesses a wide range of regional, national and local environmental data in collaboration with national bodies and expert networks. It publishes the periodic State of the European environment reports and a multitude of issue-specific assessments, helping to evaluate the effectiveness of environmental policy implementation and informing the public about environmental conditions. These activities can shape regional and national policy debates and outcomes. EEA also assists the EU fulfilling requirements under international environmental agreements, such as reporting of regional and national emissions of GHGs and other air pollutants.

The European Food Safety Authority (EFSA), created in response to a series of food scandals in the 1990s, is a risk assessment and advisory agency based in Parma since 2002. Like the EEA, EFSA does not have regulatory powers, but provides European decision makers and publics with scientific and technical information about food and feed safety, nutrition, animal health and welfare, and plant protection. EFSA plays an active role in assessing risks to the environment and human and animal health of new GMOs, where the agency's opinions inform political debate and final decisions on whether they can be placed on the single market.

The European Chemicals Agency (ECHA), located in Helsinki since 2007, fulfills several important administrative and assessment roles in the implementation of EU chemicals policy. It works closely with the European Commission, national regulatory agencies, and firms in listing all commercial chemicals in a public register. Similar to EFSA, the ECHA is instrumental in conducting environmental and human health evaluations of potentially harmful substances that play a major role in subsequent discussions and regulatory decisions.

In addition, the European Fisheries Control Agency (EFCA), located in Vigo, Spain, has been in operation since 2007. Although it has the word "control" in its title, it lacks the ability to formulate direct rules. Instead, EFCA was created to coordinate member states' operational activities pursuant to obligations outlined in the CFP, helping to strengthen EU-wide surveillance, inspection and control towards greater adherence to all fisheries-related mandates on individual member states and boat owners. This involves building governance capacities in member states, including training national inspectors seeking to stop illegal fishing beyond assigned quotas. Nevertheless, the agency's efforts have not reversed the trends plaguing many European waters of fish stocks sharply declining to seriously detrimental levels.

Lobby groups and civil society

The EU was created and expanded through intergovernmental negotiations and national governments remain critical in setting goals and adopting policy. However, EU bodies are under pressure to increase transparency and better include non-state groups and individuals in debates and decision making—an idea incorporated already in the Rome Treaty with the creation of the European Economic and Social Committee.[14] As greater authority over a larger number of policy areas moved to Brussels, more private sector and civil society groups set up shop there, focusing directly on EU bodies and policies. The European Commission has developed close ties with many of these, involving various forms of roundtable meetings and individual consultations. This has direct consequences for environmental policymaking, creating opportunities for organized interests to influence agendas and policy proposals. Many lobby groups have also increased interactions with the European Parliament, as its political importance has been elevated. Direct stakeholder interaction with the Council of the European Union remains more limited, as most lobbying of national governments takes place at the domestic level—but such lobbying can be highly influential on member state positions in Brussels.

Many perceived pros and cons about increased lobbying in Brussels are similar to debates elsewhere.[15] Inclusion of non-state groups gives business, labor unions, farmers and fishers, and environmental and public health groups opportunities to voice views on EU policies impacting them and the general public. Such stakeholder engagement opens up decision-making procedures to actors outside EU bodies and national governments, allowing interest groups to bring a wide range of perspectives and ideas to policy debates and provide policy-relevant information to decision makers. Lobbying in Brussels also provides alternative routes of influence for domestic-level groups feeling ignored by their governments, including during the transposition of environmental law. For example, Spanish advocacy groups have launched many complaints about inadequate implementation of environmental law in Spain to DG Environment, feeling their concerns are taken more seriously in Brussels than in Madrid, and hoping to use the European Commission's legal and political powers to put pressure on their national government.[16]

However, the increasingly common and expensive lobbying practices in Brussels are also subject to criticism. Institutionalized relations between the European Commission, the European Parliament, and well-organized interests mean that large and wealthy groups can have disproportionate influence on decision making. Certainly, some lobbyists have more resources and greater access to EU officials than others. Close relations between lobby groups and policymakers raise risks that narrowly focused economic interests become prioritized over more general and diffuse public goods like protecting the environment. For example, specialized interests have significant impacts on the design and operation of the CAP and the CFP, despite European farmers and fishers only representing a small portion of the overall population. These policies have been long criticized, with only limited reforms resulting due to strong resistance from deeply entrenched interests. Nevertheless, substantial lobbying efforts are now common around all major environmental issues, including climate change and renewable energy, air and water policies, and chemicals management.

To promote transparency in their relationships with advocacy groups, the European Commission and the European Parliament in 2008 established a shared online Register of Interest Representatives, building on earlier procedures in each body.[17] The 2012 annual report identified over 5,400 registered lobby groups.[18] Lobbying is dominated by industry groups such as BusinessEurope (representing national business federations in 33 countries) and large firms with generally greater financial and human resources than environmental and health advocacy groups.[19] Private sector actors have a strong interest in economic and industrial policy and the smooth functioning of the single market, giving them a direct stake in the adoption of EU environmental law when new policies seek to harmonize regulations and/or reduce trade barriers. Many industrial interests often oppose policy proposals seeking to raise pan-European standards. This was visible, for example, in aggressive private sector lobbying about recent changes to chemicals policy, where industry organizations supported efforts to streamline management practices across member states, but spent considerable resources advocating for relatively modest private sector requirements and standards.[20] Similar industry behavior is evident in much climate change and GMO policy.

Yet, industry organizations do not always take an anti-regulatory stance, and individual firms can have varied interests vis-à-vis EU environmental standard setting. Some firms may benefit from higher regional standards while others do not. For example, if a German cement producer thinks it has a comparative disadvantage compared to a Spanish competitor because German environmental mandates on pollution control and energy use are more costly to meet than those in Spain, the German firm has an interest in harmonizing standards across all member states such that all firms operate under the same regulatory regime. It may then join governments and environmental advocacy groups pushing for higher, uniform standards. Further, one industrial sector may benefit from requirements imposed on another. For example, firms mostly involved in renewable energy generation and sales may lobby for tighter GHG controls on the fossil fuel industry, if they think such controls would help them compete in national and regional energy markets.

Among environmental advocacy groups, Green 10 coordinates activities by several major environmental advocacy groups. The European Environmental Bureau plays a major umbrella role representing over 140 smaller organizations in over 30 countries. Many large organizations such as Greenpeace, Friends of the Earth and WWF International are also present in Brussels. Sometimes environmental advocacy groups receive financial support from the European Commission and/or national governments. The rationale for such funding is that environmental advocacy groups often have fewer resources than private sector organizations. To ensure broad and equitable civil society participation in policy debates, environmental groups are provided with public financial support. However, this practice is not without its critics, raising concerns that environmental advocacy groups may hesitate to express strong criticism of the European Commission and member state governments, not wanting to bite the hand that feeds them. Some environmental groups, like Greenpeace, do not accept such financial support, arguing that they do not want to give the impression that their independence could be compromised.

Growing numbers of non-European actors also operate as lobbyists in Brussels, further illustrating the rising importance of the EU in regional and international affairs. Most represent government and private sector interests. Large countries like the United States and China engage in lobbying with the European Commission, the European Parliament and national governments, expressing opinions and concerns about EU policies and new proposals on, for example, chemicals regulation, restrictions on the commercial growing and sale of GMOs, or proposed controls on GHG emissions from all airlines operating in Europe. Outside industry interests have also increased their presence. For example, the American Chamber of Commerce has a sizeable and active office in Brussels, seeking to protect the interests of its members. The European Chemical Industry Council (CEFIC) collaborates extensively with the American Chemistry Council on chemicals management issues, and many non-European airlines repeatedly spoke out against efforts to include the international airline industry in the EU GHG trading scheme, with strong backing from their national governments.

In addition, the EU created legal rights of citizens. The Charter of Fundamental Rights of the European Union, first proclaimed in 2000 and made legally binding by the Lisbon Treaty, details rights afforded to anyone living in a member state. Article 37 of the charter proclaims that "a high level of environmental protection and the improvement of the quality of the environment must be integrated into the policies of the Union and ensured in accordance with the principle of sustainable development." The charter also gives individuals the ability to petition the European Parliament to address and possibly act upon a topic— many such petitions concern environmental issues. A 2011 EU law on the so-called European Citizens' Initiative furthermore gives the public the right to petition the European Commission to develop a new policy proposal on any issue where the European Commission has authority, including the environment. Such petitions must be backed by at least one million people from at least one quarter of member states (seven out of 28), with a minimum number of needed signatories in each member state.

On the rights of individuals related to environmental governance issues, the EU was a driving force behind the adoption of the 1998 Convention on Access to Information, Public Participation in Decision-Making and Access to Justice in Environmental Matters in Aarhus, Denmark (the "Aarhus convention"). Entering into force in 2001 and part of EU law, the convention identifies three sets of rights intended to strengthen public involvement in environmental planning and decision making at both national and EU levels.[21] First, people have a right to obtain and view information held by public authorities on environmental and human health conditions and policies ("access"). Second, public authorities must provide individuals and advocacy groups with opportunities to comment on new projects, plans or programs affecting the environment, and take these comments into account when making decisions ("participation"). Third, individuals and stakeholder groups can challenge public decisions made in ways that violate the principles of access and participation, or environmental law in general ("justice").

Finally, EU law gives any person the right to initiate legal proceedings against a decision addressed to that person, or against a decision addressed to another person of "direct and individual concern," based on the argument that the decision infringes EU law. On several occasions Greenpeace and other advocacy groups have attempted to use this right to petition the European Court of Justice to take legal action on environmental provisions, decisions, or measures such as, for example, when a member state does not conduct a sufficiently detailed environmental impact assessment in violation of an EU directive. To date, however, the judges have never held such an initiative admissible; advocacy groups have not been given standing in environmental matters, as they have not been deemed directly affected and individually concerned in any way different from all other people.[22] This stand, however, does not restrict advocacy groups and individuals from taking environmental cases to domestic courts, as permitted under member states' national laws.

EU environmental policy instruments

EU law consists of primary legislation (the treaties) and secondary legislation (the many laws adopted by EU bodies, based on the authority afforded them by the treaties). Secondary legislation comes in three main forms: regulations, directives, and decisions. Regulations are passed solely by the European Commission or jointly by the Council of the European Union and the European Parliament. They are the most direct and detailed form of law and stipulate specific rules and commitments that must be implemented uniformly in all member states by a common deadline. EU bodies and member states use regulations in environmental law when they agree that a homogeneous approach is necessary, such as when the single market overlaps with environmental and human health concerns. For example, to ensure that assessment and regulation of hazardous chemicals were harmonized across member states, and to improve environmental and human health protection, the EU passed a significant new regulation with far-reaching consequences for both public and private sector actors in 2007.

While there are many regulations in EU environmental law, the more flexible directives are more common. Directives stipulate certain end results, such as reductions of sulfur dioxide emissions from large stationary sources. Member states are legally bound to meet this target, but they retain a high degree of freedom to decide which specific political and technical measures they use. Directives often specify dates by which national laws must be adopted, and may give member states differing deadlines taking into account varying national circumstances. Finally, decisions are laws relating to specific cases and are issued by the Council of the European Union (sometimes with the European

Parliament) or the European Commission. These are binding and can require authorities and individuals in member states to act or to stop doing something, and/or bestow them with specific rights. In environmental law, individual decisions exist on, for example, waste classification and handling, and air pollution data reporting and sharing.

Analysts distinguish between three broad types of EU environmental policy instruments: 1) regulatory instruments based on command and control; 2) market-based instruments such as emissions trading and eco taxes; and 3) suasive policy instruments, including voluntary agreements and eco labels.[23] Early EU environmental law relied primarily on command-and-control type of instruments in setting rules and mandates. EU environmental policy is still largely structured around such "old-style" regulatory instruments, but EU bodies have increasingly used market-based and suasive policy instruments. This change was influenced by push-back from some member states including France, Germany, and the United Kingdom against what they saw as expensive and intrusive regulatory environmental policy coming from Brussels.[24] The European Commission and member states such as Germany and the Netherlands argue that such policy methods are sometimes the most appropriate means of addressing particular environmental issues.[25]

To date, market-based and suasive policy instruments largely complement, rather than replace, command-and-control regulations within the EU. Their use definitely adds to the overall environmental policy mix, but they remain a clear minority of existing instruments.[26] The increased use of market-based and suasive policy instruments does not mean that EU bodies and national governments have lost authority and influence over environmental policy. Regional and domestic public bodies remain necessary in the formulation, implementation, review, and revisions of market-based policy instruments. Looming threats, by EU bodies and national governments, of mandatory regulation can be important to push private sector actors to conclude voluntary agreements. In addition, both EU regulatory instruments and the alternative policy instruments suffer implementation deficits, so neither type appears more effective as a general rule.

EU interest in market-based environmental policy instruments dates to the 1980s. These are often promoted by supporters as more cost-effective than command-and-control legislation, as they seek to change behavior by altering basic economic incentives.[27] The most important EU market-based environmental policy instrument is the Emissions Trading System (ETS), established in 2005 to put a price on carbon dioxide and other GHG emissions. It greatly expanded the authority of the European

Commission and other EU bodies on climate change policy, introducing a wide range of mandates—created in part due to an earlier failure by member states to establish an EU-wide carbon tax. Because member states remain protective of control over domestic taxation, the EU only managed to agree on a 2003 framework directive, harmonizing minimum tax rates for energy products. However, many member states have long histories of environmental taxation, including the use of different forms of national carbon and energy taxes.

The EU has made limited use of suasive policy instruments since the 1980s. Voluntary agreements are seen as a less rigid way to introduce mandates on private and public sector actors, compared to command-and-control legislation. The EU's ability to adopt voluntary agreements remains limited, however, as they are not explicitly recognized in the treaties. Only a few have been concluded, with industrial sectors such as the European chemicals industry. Sometimes voluntary agreements are later supplanted by binding controls. For example, the 2009 Regulation on car emissions superseded an earlier voluntary agreement with the car industry to reduce carbon dioxide emissions, dating back to 1999. Also, EU informational instruments such as a modestly successful eco-labeling scheme are designed to induce individual consumption changes through the use of logos and by making detailed product data more easily available. In addition, EU bodies express support for private sector programs such as certification schemes and broader corporate social responsibility initiatives.

EU budgets and the environment

As the EU grew in membership and scope, the annual budget increased significantly, and different programs and allocations have serious implications for environmental policy and management. The Multi-annual Financial Framework defines the EU's long-term spending priorities and sets an annual maximum budget amount that can be spent on each area (the most recent framework covers 2014–20). Almost the entire 2014 EU budget—98.9 percent—comes from three sources.[28] The first and largest is direct payments from all member states, based on a standard percentage levied on each country's gross national income (73.6 percent). Second, a standard percentage is levied on the harmonized value added tax base of each member state (13.2 percent). Customs duties on imports from outside the EU and sugar levies constitute the third source (12 percent). The remainder of the budget, just over one percent, comes from taxes on EU staff salaries, contributions from non-EU countries to certain programs, and fines on companies for breaching competition laws and other standards. The budget must balance; it is not possible to run deficits or externally borrow money to cover financial shortfalls.

The EU budget for 2014 was €142.6 billion (see Table 3.1). This may sound like a large amount, but it is relatively modest. In comparison, the UK budget for 2013 was £720 billion (approximately €850 billion), while that year's US federal budget was US$3.8 trillion (approximately €2.9 trillion). The EU 2014 budget represented around one percent of the EU-28 GDP. Put differently, each person in the 28 member states paid approximately €0.80 per day to finance the EU budget in 2014. The two largest budget sections were "sustainable growth; natural resources" and "economic, social and territorial cohesion." These involved substantial distribution of funds to different regions and countries. There are no official EU data on exactly how much money is directly spent—or where it is spent—on environment and sustainable development across the annual budgets. Definitions and opinions of what constitutes environment-related spending also differ, making such calculations difficult.

Under the largest budget item "sustainable growth; natural resources," the LIFE+ program is EU's main budget item for explicitly co-financing environmental, climate and nature conservation projects in member states and neighboring countries. At €404.6 million, it represented less than 0.5 percent of the 2014 total budget. Instead, over 75 percent of funds earmarked for this budget item (€43.8 billion) went to market-related expenditures and direct aid to support agriculture and fisheries markets; that is, subsidies to support the heavily criticized CAP and CFP. At the same time, a small amount of resources

Table 3.1 Total EU budget for 2014

Budget area	€ (million)	%
Sustainable growth; natural resources	59,267.2	41.6
Economic, social and territorial cohesion	47,502.3	33.3
Competitiveness for growth and jobs	16,484.0	11.6
Administration	8,405.1	5.9
Global Europe	8,325.0	5.8
Security and citizenship	2,172.0	1.5
Special instruments	456.2	0.4
Total	142,640.5	100

(European Commission, *Multiannual Financial Framework for 2014–2020 and EU Budget 2014: The Figures* (Brussels, 2013))

dedicated to the Structural and Cohesion Funds under the second largest budget item, "economic, social and territorial cohesion" supported environmental, energy and transport projects, such as those on improving energy efficiency, expanding renewable energy use, developing rail transport, and strengthening public transport.

Even if it is not possible to specify exactly how much of the EU budget is dedicated to environmental governance, the structure and size of budget expenditures have significant impact on ecological conditions and efforts to transition toward sustainable development. As the EU struggles to improve its environmental record, debate continues about "greening" the EU budget.[29] For example, how to move away from environmentally harmful expenditures and subsidies on agriculture and fisheries? How to design new financial instruments to promote more environmentally friendly choices and decisions by public and private sector actors? In addition, member state national budgets—and efforts to "green" these by altering taxation and fee structures to support a switch to less carbon-intensive and resource-demanding economies—in line with ecological modernization—may have significant impacts on efforts to reduce Europe's ecological footprint and bring its production and consumption within local, regional and global ecological limits.[30]

Notes

1　Andrew Jordan, Harro van Asselt, Frans Berkhout and Dave Huitema, "Understanding the Paradoxes of Multilevel Governance: Climate Change Policy in the European Union," *Global Environmental Politics* 12, no. 2 (2012): 43–66.

2　For summary discussions about main EU bodies and how they function see, for example, Michelle Cini and Nieves Pérez-Solórzano Borragán, eds, *European Union Politics*, third edn (Oxford: Oxford University Press, 2010); Desmond Dinan, *Ever Closer Union: An Introduction to European Integration* (Boulder, Col.: Lynne Rienner Publishers, 2010).

3　Rüdiger K.W. Wurzel, "Member States and the Council," in *Environmental Policy in the EU: Actors, Institutions and Processes*, ed. Andrew Jordan and Camilla Adelle, third edn (London: Earthscan, 2013), 75–94.

4　Staff data taken from: ec.europa.eu/civil_service/about/figures/index_en.htm.

5　Emmanuelle Schon-Quinlivan, "The European Commission," in *Environmental Policy in the EU: Actors, Institutions and Processes*, ed. Andrew Jordan and Camilla Adelle, third edn (London: Earthscan, 2013), 95–112.

6　Wurzel, "Member States and the Council," 75–94.

7　Simon Hix and Bjørn Høyland, "Empowerment of the European Parliament," *Annual Review of Political Science* 16 (2013): 171–89.

8　Charlotte Burns, Neil Carter and Nicholas Worsfold, "Enlargement and the Environment: Changing Behavior of the European Parliament," *Journal of Common Market Studies* 50, no. 1 (2012): 54–70.

9 Ludwig Krämer, "The European Court of Justice," in *Environmental Policy in the EU: Actors, Institutions and Processes*, ed. Andrew Jordan and Camilla Adelle, third edn (London: Earthscan, 2012), 113–31.

10 Christoph Hönnige and Diana Panke, "The Committee of the Regions and the European Economic and Social Council: How Influential are Consultative Committees in the European Union?" *Journal of Common Market Studies* 51, no. 3 (2013): 452–71.

11 Berthold Rittberger and Arndt Wonka, "Introduction: Agency Governance in the European Union," *Journal of European Public Policy* 18, no. 6 (2011): 780–89.

12 R. Daniel Kelemen and Andrew D. Tarrant, "The Political Foundation of the Eurocracy," *West European Politics* 34, no. 5 (2011): 922–47.

13 Morten Egeberg and Jarle Trondal, "EU-Level Agencies: New Executive Center Formation or Vehicles for National Control?" *Journal of European Public Policy* 18, no. 6 (2011): 868–87.

14 Irina Tanasescu, *The European Commission and Interest Groups: Towards a Deliberative Interpretation of Stakeholder Involvement in EU Policy-Making* (Brussels: VUBPRESS Brussels University Press, 2009).

15 Justin Greenwood, *Interest Representation in the European Union*, second edn (New York: Palgrave Macmillan, 2007).

16 Susana Aguilar Fernandez, "Spain: Old Habits Die Hard," in *Environmental Policy in Europe: The Europeanization of National Environmental Policy*, ed. Andrew Jordan and Duncan Liefferink (New York: Routledge, 2005).

17 Camilla Adelle and Jason Anderson, "Lobby Groups," in *Environmental Policy in the EU: Actors, Institutions and Processes*, ed. Andrew Jordan and Camilla Adelle, third edn (New York: Earthscan, 2013).

18 Joint Transparency Register Secretariat, *Annual Report on the Operations of the Transparency Register 2012* (Brussels: Joint Transparency Register Secretariat, 2012).

19 Justin Greenwood, *Interest Representation in the European Union*, second edn (New York: Palgrave Macmillan, 2007).

20 Henrik Selin, "Coalition Politics and Chemicals Management in a Regulatory Ambitious Europe," *Global Environmental Politics* 7, no. 3 (2007): 63–93.

21 Vera Rodenhoff, "The Aarhus Convention and its Implications for the 'Institutions' of the European Community," *Review of European Community and International Environmental Law* 11, no. 3 (2002): 343–57.

22 Krämer, "The European Court of Justice," 113–31.

23 Rüdiger K.W. Wurzel, Anthony R. Zito and Andrew J. Jordan, *Environmental Governance in Europe: A Comparative Analysis of New Environmental Policy Instruments* (Northampton, Mass.: Edward Elgar, 2013).

24 Andrew Jordan, David Benson, Rüdiger K.W. Wurzel and Anthony Zito, "Governing with Multiple Policy Instruments?" in *Environmental Policy in the EU: Actors, Institutions and Processes*, ed. Andrew Jordan and Camilla Adelle, third edn (New York: Earthscan, 2013).

25 European Commission, *Communication from the Commission to the European Parliament, the Council, the Economic and Social Committee and the Committee of the Regions—Environmental Agreements at Community Level—Within the Framework of the Action Plan on the Simplification and Improvement of the Regulatory Environment, COM* (2002), 0412 (Brussels,

2002); Rüdiger K.W. Wurzel, "Germany: From Environmental Leadership to Partial Mismatch," in *Environmental Policy in Europe: The Europeanization of National Environmental Policy*, ed. Andrew Jordan and Duncan Liefferink (New York: Routledge, 2005); Duncan Liefferink and Marielle Van Der Zouwen, "The Netherlands: The Advantages of Being 'Mr Average'," in *Environmental Policy in Europe: The Europeanization of National Environmental Policy*, ed. Andrew Jordan and Duncan Liefferink (New York: Routledge, 2005).

26   Wurzel *et al.*, *Environmental Governance in Europe*.

27   Winston Harrington, Richard D. Morgenstern and Thomas Sterner, eds, *Choosing Environmental Policy: Comparing Instruments and Outcomes in the United States and Europe* (Washington, DC: Resources for the Future, 2004).

28   European Commission, *Multiannual Financial Framework for 2014–2020 and EU Budget 2014: The Figures* (Brussels, 2013).

29   David Baldock, Keti Medarova-Bergström and Axel Volkery, *The Post-2013 Multiannual Financial Framework: Time to Be Bolder* (Brussels: Institute for European Environmental Policy, 2011).

30   J. Peter Clinch, Kai Schlegelmilch, Rolf-Ulrich Sprenger and Ursula Triebswetter, *Greening the Budget: Budgetary Policies for Environmental Improvement* (Northampton, Mass.: Edward Elgar, 2002).

4 Analyzing environmental decision making and implementation

- Guiding principles for environmental governance
- Setting agendas and formulating policy options
- Adopting new environmental policy
- Implementing and enforcing environmental policy

The EU is a highly consensus-oriented organization. The individuals who work within the EU representing different bodies and member states value this approach. Despite this deep-rooted preference for compromise, many political disagreements and struggles for influence exist at any given time. Sometimes this involves major issues such as the formulation of treaty provisions outlining the rights and obligations of different EU bodies on environmental and other issues, potentially including substantial transfer of authority from national governments, parliaments and courts to the supranational level. At other times, controversies focus on specific policy issues and on exactly which rules and standards are most appropriate. For example, how best to regulate sulfur dioxide or mercury emissions from stationary sources, if a new GMO should be approved for planting or use in food and feed, or what constitutes a technically, economically and environmentally appropriate GHG reduction goal for an individual member state or the EU as a whole.

As in any political system, analyzing EU environmental law making and implementation requires paying attention to both formal procedures and informal processes. This chapter focuses on the decision-making and implementation system governed by the Lisbon Treaty. The chapter first highlights several guiding principles for EU environmental governance. The next section discusses processes of setting agendas and the formulation of environmental policy options, led by the European Commission in interaction with a large number of other stakeholders. This is followed by a closer look at the adoption of environmental policy through the ordinary legislative procedure, once the European Commission issues a formal proposal, involving close interactions between the Council of the European Union and the European Parliament. The final section examines critical aspects of environmental policy implementation and enforcement, where the European Commission, the Court of Justice, and member states all play key roles.

Guiding principles for environmental governance

In theory, EU activities and environmental decision making are guided by a set of broad principles, articulated in EU treaties and laws, EAPs, and European Commission documents. Five stand out as particularly prominent:

1   the polluter pays principle;
2   the precautionary principle;
3   the subsidiarity and proportionality principles; and
4   the effort sharing principle.

The legal status and specific application of these principles developed over time, through amendments to EU treaties, political changes in relationships among EU bodies and member states, final language in adopted laws, and pioneering rulings by the Court of Justice.[1] At the same time, environmental policymaking and implementation offer substantial evidence of the difficulty in moving from general political agreement to successful application and integration of core principles into the everyday activities of EU bodies and member states.

The importance of the polluter pays principle was recognized in the first EAP in 1973. It remains a core principle in environmental policy around the world, at least rhetorically, and was legally recognized as a central principle of EU law in the SEA.[2] Simply put, it stipulates that polluters should bear the financial burden of pollution reduction and clean-up actions. Related to this, the Council of the European Union and the European Parliament in 2004 passed a separate directive on environmental liability.[3] The directive's preamble states that "an operator whose activity has caused the environmental damage or the imminent threat of such damage is to be held financially liable, in order to induce operators to adopt measures and develop practices to minimise the risks of environmental damage so that their exposure to financial liabilities is reduced." Consequently, this directive creates a legal framework for how to remedy situations where harm has occurred as well as lays down stipulations for the prevention of environmental damage at its source. It seeks, in other words, to enact the polluter pays principle into enforceable law.

Connecting back to the importance of preventative action discussed in the first EAP, the first legally binding EU formulation of the precautionary principle resides in the Maastricht Treaty, which states that it should guide all EU environmental policymaking.[4] The precautionary principle stipulates that a lack of scientific certainty shall not be used as a reason to postpone cost-effective measures to prevent environmental degradation, where threats of serious or irreversible damage exist. That is, environmental protection measures should be taken in the face of scientific uncertainty if there may be severe risks. In 2000, the European Commission issued a communication attempting to promote a common understanding of the precautionary principle and establish broader guidelines for its application.[5] This recognizes that the Maastricht Treaty only prescribes the precautionary principle to environmental issues, but argues that it should be considered across environmental, human, animal and plant health issues. This interpretation is supported by Court of Justice rulings expanding the principle's scope to include human health. Integration of precaution into EU environmental and health policy, however, is uneven at best.[6]

The subsidiarity principle was enshrined in the Maastricht Treaty, and linked to the simultaneous creation of the Committee of the Regions. It stipulates that decisions should be taken at the lowest appropriate administrative level, and it is intended to provide guidance as to when an issue falls under EU authority and when it is better addressed at national or local levels. The Lisbon Treaty confirms the right of the Committee of Regions to bring an action before the Court of Justice if it believes that an EU law violates the subsidiarity principle. The European Commission's environmental impact assessment guidelines state that two questions related to the subsidiary principle should be asked when considering a new policy proposal (see also below).[7] First, why can the objectives of the proposed action not be sufficiently achieved by the member states (a necessity test)? Second, can objectives be better achieved by EU action (an EU value added test)? Subsidiarity is also closely related to the principle of proportionality, which declares that EU action should not go beyond what is necessary to achieve set EU objectives.

Finally, the effort sharing principle, sometimes called burden sharing, is critical in EU environmental goal setting and law making. Its application is seen in air pollution, climate change, and energy policies. Rather than assigning each member state the same numerical target, states may differ in their responsibilities (or requirements) in support of a collective EU target. For example, a 2009 effort sharing decision set out an EU-wide 10 percent reduction (from 2005 levels, by 2020) in GHG emissions from sources not included in the ETS, broken into differing national targets based on GDP per capita.[8] Member states with relatively high GDP per capita are required to reduce their GHG emissions more than those with lower GDP per capita—some can even increase emissions, as national targets range from 20 percent reductions to 20 percent increases. The provision of assistance to less developed member states and regions to support meeting environmental mandates is also based on effort sharing ideas. The assignment of individual national targets remains controversial, however, as member states sometimes seek to limit their own commitments.

Setting agendas and formulating policy options

As in any open and complex political system, a huge number of public, private and civil society actors interact to shape the EU agenda on environmental issues. Agenda setting around environmental issues involves identification of anthropogenic environmental problems, making a particular issue a discussion topic, and then getting it seen as an action item.[9] This calls attention to the scientific and technical information often involved in identifying a phenomenon as an anthropogenic impact, as well as the construction of such impacts as a "problem." Thus, agenda setting in environmental politics includes research and knowledge production (with an accompanying construction of causal understandings), as well as social framing processes among a host of diverse actors.[10] It involves assessing how issues are introduced into discussions among actors of all types, and how they move from debates to items associated with specific policy actions.

Around many environmental issues, like air and water pollution and toxic substances, agenda-setting processes began in earnest in the late 1960s and early 1970s. The initiative for a new environmental law, or strengthening an existing one, can originate from many different actors and be driven by a multitude of organized groups and interests, but member states often play a central role. Occasionally, an environmental issue gets pushed up the political agenda as a result of actions at the very highest political level in the European Council. Then it may matter which member state holds the Presidency, as some countries take more active interest in specific environmental issues than others.[11] However, member states are more likely to act through the Council of the European Union where a simple majority, often led by green leader states, can request that the European Commission launch a study into the possible need for legislative changes. The European Parliament also organizes debates around specific environmental issues such as GHG controls, GMOs and water quality, and can, by a majority of MEPs, ask the European Commission to examine whether policy changes are warranted.

Many processes, however, start within the European Commission, which has the formal "right of initiative" and can launch its own initiatives aimed at harmonizing or changing standards, for example because member states have different national standards impacting the operation of the single market. Alternatively, DG Environment, DG Climate Action, or another unit within the European Commission may believe that existing regional standards should be strengthened and/or better implemented. Such initiatives are sometimes taken in response to growing scientific and technical evidence, involving work by the EEA and other specialized agencies. Moreover, industry organizations and environmental and other types of advocacy groups often seek to shape EU policy debates and agendas by promoting their perspectives and regulatory interests either directly to EU bodies, including through the formulation of opinions in the European Economic and Social Committee, or via member states. Individuals influence agenda setting and the work of the European Commission through the petition system set up through the European Citizens' Initiative.

Once an environmental policy issue arrives on the European Commission's agenda, most fall under the auspices of DG Environment. Since 2010, however, climate change issues are handled by DG Climate Action—the creation of which partly reflects the size and complexity of climate change policy issues, as well as an attempt to engender greater policy integration among related issue areas of environmental protection, energy generation and use, transportation standards and planning, and industrial production. Furthermore, GMOs are placed under DG Health and Consumers, agricultural issues are assigned to DG Agriculture and Rural Development, while fisheries issues are the responsibility of DG Maritime Affairs and Fisheries. Environmental advocates often complain that the "non-environmental" DGs place a lower priority on environmental and sustainability goals, in favor of traditional economic priorities and industry interests. Yet, even when one DG is assigned the lead position, policy draft proposals are typically subject to extensive discussion across multiple DGs, since environmental issues cut across many policy areas and all units of the European Commission must collectively back a final proposal.

Under EU treaties, the European Commission is formally tasked with promoting common European interests, rather than national ones, but Commissioners and DG staff often express diverging perspectives on such interests and related policy proposals. DGs cover varying political and economic interests in European integration, and frequently interact with different sets of stakeholder groups. For example, DG Environment has relatively close ties with the EU specialized agencies covering environmental issues, member state environment ministries and regulatory agencies, and major environmental advocacy groups. In fact, it is common for DG staff members to be former national ministerial or environmental advocacy group employees—and many have professional training related to natural environmental science and engineering or environmental law. Meanwhile, DG Industry or DG Internal Market personnel often work more closely with industry and business organizations. Such differences in focus and engagement with organized interests can result in politically contentious disagreements within the European Commission before all Commissioners reach agreement.

The European Commission frequently engages outside actors during the formulation of policy proposals, as DG staff rely on external information and technical expertise to prepare detailed and technically complicated draft laws. The European Commission is also required to consult with local and regional authorities through the Committee of the Regions. Although this committee has mere consultative status and cannot reject a proposal, it issues "opinions" on all environmental, climate change, and energy policy proposals. Member state representatives may also play extensive roles in formulating new policy through the designation of national experts to DGs, paid by their home governments to work on particular issues. On air pollution, for example, British, German and Swedish government officials placed within DG Environment shaped major policy proposals on reducing emissions of sulfur dioxide, nitrous oxide, and volatile organic compounds (VOCs).[12]

In 2002, the European Commission introduced the use of impact assessments to evaluate positive and negative impacts of environmental policy options before proposals are formally issued. Based on 2009 guidelines, the impact assessment for each policy option should follow a set formula consisting of six consecutive steps related to carrying out the necessity and EU value added tests mentioned earlier with respect to the application of the subsidiarity principle: 1) identify the nature and extent of the problem, including key players and major drivers and underlying causes, and determine if the problem falls within the EU's remit to act; 2) define general, specific, and operational policy objectives clearly linked to the problem and its root causes; 3) establish which policy options and delivery mechanisms are most likely to achieve identified objectives; 4) analyze economic, social, and environmental impacts including potential trade-offs and synergies; 5) compare all relevant positive and negative impacts of each policy option; and 6) consider arrangements for future policy monitoring and evaluation.[13]

Impact assessments are intended to help formulate better policy, also linked to environmental policy integration efforts. While impact assessments influence the collaborative work across DGs and proposals put forward, the reports seem to play a limited role in the subsequent decision-making phase involving the Council of the European Union and the European Parliament. They are rarely used in follow-up assessments of approved legislation.[14] In addition, the European Commission increasingly engages in open, online reviews of draft policy proposals, where comments are publicly available. This constitutes a relatively recent attempt to make the process more transparent and provide individuals, member states, and advocacy groups with another opportunity to shape the formulation of policy proposals. In addition, non-European states and stakeholder groups offer views on policy initiatives affecting them through trade with the EU or other transnational mechanisms, as seen during the development of recent chemicals laws and discussions about regulating GHGs from the international airline industry.[15]

Adopting new environmental policy

Under the ordinary legislative procedure (see Figure 4.1), the European Commission submits an environmental policy proposal endorsed by the full College of Commissioners together with the impact assessment report to member states' national parliaments, which have eight weeks to issue a reasoned opinion on whether they believe the proposal complies with the subsidiarity principle. If one third say no, the proposal must be reviewed by the European Commission to consider changes. If a simple majority of national parliaments believe the proposal violates the subsidiarity principle, the European Parliament and the Council of the European Union must consider this issue when they review the draft legal act. The proposal and impact assessment report are also sent to the Committee of the Regions, and may also go to the Economic and Social Committee if the topic relates to issues falling under its area of competence. Most importantly, however, the two documents simultaneously go to the European Parliament and the Council of the European Union for deliberation during their respective first readings (where there is no set time line for how soon the two bodies need to act).

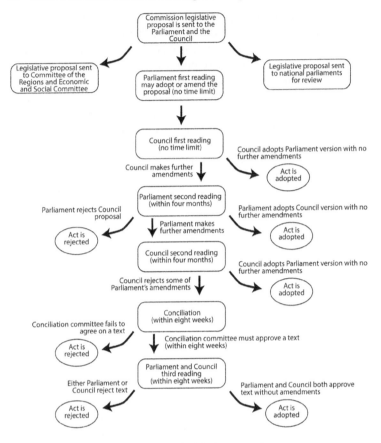

Figure 4.1 Outline of the ordinary legislative procedure

In the European Parliament, MEPs may adopt the European Commission's proposal or, more likely, introduce amendments. Most of this work occurs in a lead committee where an environmental policy proposal is taken up in the Committee on Environment, Public Health and Food Safety, while agricultural and fisheries issues are addressed in their respective committees. Temporary committees, such as the 2007–09 one on climate change to develop the Climate Change and Energy package, can also be established.[16] The committee reviews the proposal under the leadership of a designated rapporteur, and may also organize hearings with outside experts. All amendments are voted on in committee before being sent to plenary, where additional amendments may be proposed by other committees, political groups, or groups of at least

40 MEPs. In both committee and plenary, a simple majority of voting members is required to approve an amendment. During this process, there is normally much communication with the European Commission and the Council of the European Union offering their opinions of amendments considered by the MEPs. The European Parliament can also consult the Committee of the Regions and the Economic and Social Committee.

Following the plenary vote in the European Parliament, the Council of the European Union, having started its preparatory work in parallel with the MEPs reviewing and acting on the proposal, must produce a common position. The Environment Council deals with environmental issues, including climate change. Agricultural and fisheries-related issues are sent to the Agriculture and Fisheries Council. The Council of the European Union must also inform the Committee of the Regions and the Economic and Social Committee of its work. Before a policy proposal gets debated and formally agreed by national ministers, the legal dossier is examined in lower-level working groups and committees. Working groups, consisting of mid-level civil servants from national governments or their permanent missions in Brussels, do most of the work, reviewing the version of the proposal coming out of the European Parliament's first reading and seeking as much agreement among member states as possible on whether or not new amendments should be introduced. Here member state leader/laggard dynamics regarding preferred environmental standards often come into play.

After working group review, the dossier including any unresolved issues is passed to the Committee of Permanent Representatives, consisting of member states' permanent representatives to the EU (holding the formal title of ambassadors). Meetings are chaired by the member state holding the Presidency of the European Council. After negotiations on outstanding issues, the dossier passes to the national government ministers working through the Environment Council and the Agriculture and Fisheries Council. They agree on a common position based on either the Lisbon Treaty's double majority system for qualified majority voting or the older qualified majority system (up until 2017, at the latest). No matter the voting formula, member states typically strive to make decisions by consensus. There are no official EU data, but one estimate claims that 70 percent of dossiers are settled at the working group level, while 85–90 percent of issues are addressed by the time they leave the Committee of Permanent Representatives— not requiring any further ministerial negotiations.[17] Also, when one or a few countries do not have enough votes to block a decision, they may not force a vote they know they will lose.

If the Council of the European Union and the European Parliament agree on an identical proposal—that is, if they both accept the European Commission's original proposal, or adopt the same amendments—it becomes law. In such instances, many informal meetings between representatives of the three bodies typically occur to ensure that an act is adopted following the first reading (so-called "trilogues"). When disagreements persist, the European Parliament, in both committee and plenary, must conduct a second reading within four months, during which MEPs can accept, reject, or amend the Council of the European Union's common position. If the common position is accepted by simple majority (or if MEPs fail to act within the time limit), it becomes law. If it is rejected by an absolute majority, the process ends and no law is adopted—which almost never happens. If MEPs introduce further amendments by an absolute majority, the legislative process continues. In all of these cases, both the European Commission and the Council of the European Union are in frequent contact with MEPs, expressing their opinions on actions considered by the European Parliament.

The Council of the European Union, during its second reading going through the hierarchy of committees, must accept or reject by qualified majority the European Parliament's proposal within four months. If member states accept the European Parliament's version without change, the law is adopted. If member states reject the European Parliament's amendments, a Conciliation Committee consisting of equal numbers of members from the two bodies is created within eight weeks, tasked with developing a compromise text. Typically during this stage many informal trilogue negotiations take place, bringing the European Commission into the discussions. If the Conciliation Committee does not reach a compromise within eight weeks of its creation, the legislative process ends. If the Conciliation Committee approves a compromise text, it is simultaneously presented to the Council of the European Union and the European Parliament. Both bodies, through qualified majority and simple majority in plenary, respectively, must make final decisions within eight weeks in a third reading. If both approve the text (no further amendments can be made), the law is adopted. If either body rejects the proposal, or does not act in time, it fails.

Failure to reach agreement during the ordinary legislative procedure is extremely rare, despite sometimes difficult negotiations between MEPs and member states with active European Commission involvement and political pressure from external groups, illustrating the EU's strong consensus focus. In fact, recent years have seen a growing trend toward early agreement, in most cases by the end of the first reading. During the 2004–09 session of the European Parliament, 72 percent of files subject to the ordinary legislative procedure were approved after the first reading, 23 percent following the second reading, and 5 percent after the third reading. Twenty percent of all these cases were environmental.[18] During the 2009–14 legislative session, as many as 89 percent of all cases going through the ordinary legislative procedure were settled after the first reading. About 10 percent were finalized at the end of the second reading, and only 1 percent went through the third reading.[19]

Implementing and enforcing environmental policy

Implementation refers to the actions taken by EU bodies and member states intended to meet requirements, goals and standards outlined in EU primary and secondary legislation. Implementation challenges and associated enforcement issues have loomed large in EU governance since the beginning of EEC environmental policymaking, and have grown substantially with increases in membership and the quantity and stringency of environmental law. Already the fourth EAP identified the need to improve implementation as a central challenge, and subsequent EAPs have continued to express growing concerns about an ongoing lack of implementation of much EU environmental law. The need to address the enduring implementation deficits in member states is also a central message in the periodic State of the European Environment reports, and other EEA and European Commission reports over the years.

Ultimately, each member state is responsible for timely transposition of new environmental laws as well as the continuous correct application of existing ones within its territory. In analyzing EU policy implementation and enforcement mechanisms, it is important to recognize that member states developed their own distinct legal and political systems over many generations, and that a large number of national environmental (and economic and social) policies were already in place when EU laws and standards were developed.[20] Non-compliance with EU law can be intentional (member states actively choosing not to comply with a law they see as unimportant or disagree with) or more unintentional (member states making a serious effort to comply, but failing due to political, economic, technical, or administrative factors). Consequently, member state responses are shaped by two broad sets of national factors that differ across countries: First, their policy preferences and the degree to which they support the EU policy; and second, their capacities, related in part to the degree of institutional fit between EU standards and domestic structures.[21]

The European Commission monitors member state implementation and initiate enforcement measures as necessary. With over 500 environmental regulations, directives, and decisions to oversee across 28 member states, the task is Herculean. The European Commission's over 30,000 employees may sound like a large bureaucracy, but it is heavily dependent on outside expertise and resources to monitor implementation. For information, it relies largely on member state self-reporting, and on data from EEA and direct complaints from civil society groups, firms, and individuals. In 2011, for example, 3,115 new complaints regarding insufficient domestic implementation across all areas of EU policy were filed with the European Commission, most against Italy (386), Spain (306), and Germany (263). Environmental complaints constituted the single largest group of these: 604 of the 3,115.[22] Each year also includes many environment-related petitions to the European Parliament.[23] Even if most of these do not concern direct violation of EU law, they reflect public concern about issues such as waste management, impact assessments, and air and water pollution.[24]

The infringement procedure

The infringement procedure is the European Commission's main legal and political means of overseeing implementation and engaging member states on compliance issues, applying to all policy areas of exclusive and shared competence. It is carried out through four discrete stages. First, the European Commission informally contacts the national government of a member state it believes is not meeting its obligations to open discussion. This may involve the European Commission conducting on-site spot investigations. These are rare in environmental cases, but more common in issues such as competition and fisheries. If the European Commission is satisfied by the outcome of the informal discussions, including the member state's actions to address the situation, the process ends. Otherwise, the European Commission may proceed to the second phase: sending written formal notice to the member state summarizing the situation and requesting that it submits an official response within a given time.

If the European Commission is satisfied with a member state's response to its formal letter, the issue is resolved. If the European Commission finds the response unsatisfactory, it moves to the third phase, producing a reasoned opinion. This document outlines the European Commission's position on the alleged infringement, and requests member state compliance with specified requirements within a set time. If the member state fails to meet these requests, the European

Commission may refer the case to the Court of Justice, but most infringement cases are closed before this happens. In the fourth phase, the Court of Justice rules on whether the member state is in breach of its obligations. A member state found to be non-compliant must take all necessary measures to fulfill its duties. If a member state fails to comply with the ruling, the European Commission can apply to the Court of Justice a second time, including asking for financial penalties. The average total time from the European Commission's first informal action to a final legal ruling is almost four years, where the average duration of an environmental court case is approximately two years.

There are no official Court of Justice statistics on environmental infringement cases specifically, but Krämer estimates that judges issued over 700 judgments on environmental issues between 1976 and 2010.[25] About 75 percent of these were cases initiated by the European Commission. In most other instances national courts asked for a preliminary judgment on domestic cases involving EU law. No case has been brought by one member state against another for failing to implement environmental law. The European Commission has discretionary powers to decide whether to bring cases to the Court of Justice, often submitting only cases it believes it has a high probability of winning. Many of the rulings over the years are seen by legal observers to be pro-environment, meaning that judges often back positions by EU bodies calling for more stringent implementation of environmental law over those of individual member states. By 2011, financial penalties had been used against member states in only three environmental cases: Greece (1997), Spain (2001), and France (2007).[26] In 2012, the Court of Justice issued financial penalties against Ireland in two cases relating to inadequate use of impact assessment and waste management.[27]

European Commission data show a recent decline in open infringement cases across all areas of EU law, from almost 2,900 cases in 2009, to 2,100 in 2010, 1,775 in 2011 and 1,343 by the end of 2012.[28] When compared across the main EU policy areas, the environmental area had the single highest number of infringement cases open in late 2012: 272 cases, or 20 percent of the total. Many concerned insufficient member state implementation of fully adopted legislation and were launched either on the European Commission's initiative, or as a result of external complaints. Other cases were initiated by the European Commission for member state failure to transpose newly adopted directives into domestic law by set deadlines (so-called "late transposition"). Recent environmental infringement cases cover a wide range of issue areas, with those having the highest number in 2012 being water management, nature protection, waste handling, inadequate application of impact assessments, and air quality. By the end of 2012, member states had still not implemented 35 court judgments on environmental issues, exposing themselves to future financial penalties.

The 2012 numbers of environment-related infringement procedures furthermore would be higher were climate change, with 35 open cases, not treated as a separate issue area. There were also 93 ongoing cases on energy and 26 cases on agriculture and rural development. Since many of these additional cases have clear relationships to ecological quality and sustainable development, seeking to enforce implementation of environment-related policies in member states is a major topic for the European Commission and the EU generally. In addition, the number of infringement procedures varies substantially across member states and over time, but in recent years many of the same countries had the most open in the environment area (not including climate change, energy, or other connected areas). In 2011, Italy (33), Greece (24) and Spain (23) had the highest numbers of open environmental cases. In 2012, that list was topped by Spain (27), followed by Italy (25) and Greece (19). At the same time, the European Commission in 2012 launched procedures against 24 out of 27 member states for failure to transpose a directive on buildings' energy performance.[29]

The comitology procedure

The awkwardly named comitology procedure is a second process through which the European Commission and member states engage policy implementation issues.[30] EU environmental laws, frequently broad and complex, often require extensive specification after their initial adoption, and this process is an intricate mixture of legal, political, and technocratic aspects of decision making. Even if not outlined in the Rome Treaty, the comitology system emerged in the 1960s when the member states realized that due to the growing body of EU secondary legislation, they increasingly lacked the resources to effectively make all necessary implementation rules. The Council of the European Union began to delegate implementing powers to this process and, as a system for the member states to supervise this process, the comitology procedure was established. Comitology rules have changed multiple times. A first formal comitology decision was adopted by member states in 1987, as the SEA gave comitology a clear legal foundation. Following the Lisbon Treaty, the current comitology system is mandated in a 2011 comitology regulation (replacing an earlier 1999 Council decision).[31]

The current regulation stipulates that the European Commission proposes so-called "implementing acts" pursuant to existing laws through either an examination procedure or an advisory procedure. All issues relating to the CAP, the CFP, the environment, and the health or safety of humans, animals or plants fall under the examination procedure. Then the European Commission drafts a proposed implementing act, sometimes in close collaboration with a specialized agency. This is submitted to a comitology committee consisting of lower-level representatives of all member states and chaired by a European Commission official. The committee expresses an opinion on the proposal via qualified majority (where the chair does not take part in the vote). If the comitology committee's opinion is positive—i.e. there is at least a qualified majority in favor—the draft implementing act is adopted. If the comitology committee issues a negative opinion—i.e. there is at least a qualified majority against—the proposal fails. If the committee cannot reach a qualified majority for or against the proposal, this results in a no opinion, giving the European Commission discretion over whether to adopt it—possibly putting the European Commission right in the middle of member state controversies such as GMO approvals.

If after a negative opinion, the European Commission still thinks that an implementing act is necessary, or if the European Commission does not want to adopt a proposal following a no opinion, it has two options. It may revise the original proposal and submit an amended version to the same comitology committee, starting the process over, or re-submit the original proposal to an appeal committee, where any member state or the chair may suggest amendments as a way to find agreement. If the appeal committee's opinion is positive, the European Commission adopts the original proposal; if the opinion is negative, the European Commission cannot adopt the implementing act and the process ends. If the appeal committee delivers no opinion, the European Commission again has the authority to decide whether to adopt it. The European Commission is required to send information relating to all comitology proceedings to the European Parliament, but it only has the right to inform the European Commission if it thinks that a draft proposal exceeds the implementation powers given the European Commission under the original legal act.[32]

As EU environmental law expanded and the European Commission was granted more implementation powers, the importance of the comitology procedure increased substantially, blurring the line between policymaking and implementation. Many critical decisions are not taken during the relatively transparent ordinary legislative procedure, but during little-publicized meetings of non-elected officials in comitology committees. To increase transparency of a quite opaque process, all committees are identified in an online registry and their activities are summarized in annual reports by the European Commission.[33] Recently, 200–300 comitology committees were in operation in a given year. In 2011, 268 comitology committees were organized in 29 policy sectors.[34] Reflecting the significance of environmental law within the EU, environment policies had the second highest number of committees, at 30. In addition, there were four climate action committees, 14 agriculture and rural development committees, and five maritime affairs and fisheries committees. This extensive and growing use of comitology raises serious concerns about efforts to increase EU policymaking openness and repeated attempts to make the EU more democratic.

The Lisbon Treaty introduced a second means of granting the European Commission authority over updating secondary legislation, so-called "delegated acts."[35] These "supplement or amend certain non-essential elements" of laws adopted through co-decision. This may, for example, involve making changes to a pollution-control annex—something that can be highly political. Here, the European Commission submits a proposed change simultaneously to the Council of the European Union and the European Parliament. The act enters into force only if neither the Council of the European Union (by qualified majority) nor the European Parliament (by absolute majority) objects. This newer system puts the two bodies on equal footing in reviewing proposals by the European Commission, with each body also holding the right to revoke the European Commission's power of delegation on specific issues at any time. Whether a specific part of a law is revised through implementing or delegated acts is stipulated in the original text. MEPs often advocate for delegated over implementing acts, arguing the former are more democratic and also seeking to enhance their influence. Because this important choice of procedure is subjective, it can cause discord between the European Parliament and member states seeking to protect their authority during initial law-making.

Notes

1   Ludwig Krämer, "The European Court of Justice," in *Environmental Policy in the EU: Actors, Institutions and Processes*, ed. Andrew Jordan and Camilla Adelle, third edn (London: Earthscan, 2012), 113–31.
2   James A. Tobey and Henri Smets, "The Polluter-Pays Principle in the Context of Agriculture and the Environment," *The World Economy* 19, no. 1 (2007): 63–87.
3   Council Directive 2004/35/CE on environmental liability with regard to the prevention and remedying of environmental damage, 21 April 2004.

4 Noelle Eckley and Henrik Selin, "All Talk, Little Action: Precaution and its Effects on European Chemicals Regulation," *Journal of European Public Policy* 11, no. 1 (2004): 78–105.

5 Commission Communication from the European Commission on the Precautionary Principle (Brussels, 2000).

6 European Environment Agency, *Late Lessons from Early Warnings: Science, Precaution, Innovation* (Copenhagen, 2013).

7 European Commission, *Impact Assessment Guidelines, SEC (2009) 92* (Brussels, 2009).

8 Parliament and Council Decision no. 406/2009/EC on the effort of Member States to reduce their greenhouse gas emissions to meet the Community's greenhouse gas emission reduction commitments up to 2020, 2009.

9 Ronald B. Mitchell, *International Politics and the Environment* (London: Sage Publications, 2010).

10 Stacy D. VanDeveer, "Agenda Setting at Sea and in the Air," in *Improving Global Environmental Governance: Best Practices for Architecture and Agency*, ed. Norichika Kanie, Steinar Andresen, and Peter M. Haas (London: Routledge, 2014), 31–55.

11 Rüdiger K.W. Wurzel, "The Role of the EU Presidency in the Environmental Field: Does it Make a Difference Which State Runs the Presidency?" *Journal of European Public Policy* 3, no. 2 (1996): 272–91.

12 Henrik Selin and Stacy D. VanDeveer, "Institutional Linkages and European Air Pollution Politics," in *Governing the Air: The Dynamics of Science, Policy and Citizen Interaction*, ed. R. Lidskog and G. Sundqvist (Cambridge, Mass.: MIT Press, 2011), 61–92.

13 Commission Communication, Guidelines SEC (2009) 92.

14 Camilla Adelle, Andrew Jordan and John Turnpenny, "Policy Making," in *Environmental Policy in the EU: Actors, Institutions and Processes*, ed. Andrew Jordan and Camilla Adelle, third edn (New York: Earthscan, 2013).

15 Henrik Selin, "Coalition Politics and Chemicals Management in a Regulatory Ambitious Europe," *Global Environmental Politics* 7, no. 3 (2007): 63–93.

16 Charlotte Burns, "The European Parliament," in *Environmental Policy in the EU: Actors, Institutions and Processes*, ed. Andrew Jordan and Camilla Adelle, third edn (New York: Earthscan, 2013).

17 Fiona Hayes-Renshaw and Helen Wallace, *The Council of Ministers*, second edn (Basingstoke: Palgrave Macmillan, 2006).

18 European Parliament, *Activity Report 1 May 2004 to 13 July 2009 of the Delegations to the Conciliation Committee* (Brussels, 2009).

19 European Parliament, *Directorate for Plenary Sessions, Legislative Procedures Voted in Plenary 7th Parliamentary Term 2009–14* (2014).

20 Andrew Jordan and Duncan Liefferink, eds, *Environmental Policy in Europe: The Europeanization of National Environmental Policy* (New York: Routledge, 2005).

21 Tanja A. Börzel, "Pace-setting, Foot-dragging and Fence-sitting: Member State Responses to Europeanization," *Journal of Common Market Studies* 40, no. 2 (2002): 193–214.

22 European Commission, *29th Annual Report on Monitoring the Application of EU Law* (Brussels, 2011).

23 Individuals, either alone or as a group, may submit a petition to the European Parliament on an issue covered by the EU, including the environment. A

petition may take the form of a complaint or a request and may relate to issues of public or private interest. A petition gives the European Parliament the opportunity of calling attention to any infringement of an individual's rights. See Ludwig Krämer, "The Environmental Complaint in EU Law," *Journal for European Environmental & Planning Law* 6, no. 1 (2009): 13–35.

24 European Commission, *27th Annual Report on Monitoring the Application of EU Law, COM (2010) 538* (2010).
25 Krämer, "The European Court of Justice," 113–31.
26 Andrew Jordan and Jale Tosun, "Policy Implementation," in *Environmental Policy in the EU: Actors, Institutions and Processes*, ed. Andrew Jordan and Camilla Adelle, third edn (New York: Earthscan, 2013).
27 European Commission, *30th Annual Report on Monitoring the Application of EU Law* (2012).
28 European Commission, *30th Annual Report on Monitoring the Application of EU Law* (2012).
29 European Commission, *30th Annual Report on Monitoring the Application of EU Law* (2012).
30 The origin of the use of the word "comitology" in the EU is unclear. C. Northcote Parkinson in his book *Parkinson's Law*, published in 1958, introduced the phrase "the science of comitology" for the study of how committees work. However, it may also be that comitology has more to do with the word "comity" as in "a comity of nations." As one report from the UK House of Lords noted, however, whatever the origin, "it has become an example, par excellence, of Euro-speak." House of Lords, the Select Committee on the European Union, *Reforming Comitology*, Session 2002–03, 31 Report (2003), 7.
31 Council Regulation 182/2011 of the European Parliament and of the Council of 16 February 2011 laying down the rules and general principles concerning mechanisms for control by Member States of the Commission's exercise of implementing powers.
32 Jens Blom-Hansen, "The EU Comitology System: Taking Stock Before the New Lisbon Regime," *Journal of European Public Policy* 18, no. 4 (2011): 607–17.
33 See ec.europa.eu/transparency/regcomitology/index.cfm.
34 European Commission, *Report from the Commission on the Working of Committees During 2011, COM (2012) 685* (Brussels, 2012).
35 Alan Hardacre and Michael Kaeding. *Delegated & Implementing Acts: The New Comitology. European Institute of Public Administration* (Maastricht, 2013).

5 Cases in European environmental governance

- **Air policy**
- **Water policy**
- **Waste management**
- **Chemicals management**
- **Genetically modified organisms (GMOs)**
- **The Common Agricultural Policy (CAP)**
- **The Common Fisheries Policy (CFP)**
- **Biodiversity protection**
- **Climate change and renewable energy**
- **Increased standards and mixed outcomes**

EU environmental governance addresses a multitude of legal, political, scientific, and technical issues at regional, national, and local levels simultaneously. Individual issue areas include a host of policy goals, regulations, directives, decisions, programs and other initiatives influencing behavior and choices of member states and actors within them. Many environmental policies also apply to the four EFTA countries (Iceland, Lichtenstein, Norway and Switzerland). In several areas, EU bodies and member states are trying to combine and streamline legislation to clarify obligations and rights for public, private, and civil society actors. Many initiatives seek to raise regional standards for environmental and human health protection and push European societies toward greater sustainability. At 40-something, EU environmental policy has achieved substantial institutional innovation, policy implementation, and increased stringency in some areas and cases, with only limited success identifiable in others.

As earlier chapters make clear, much environmental legislation from the 1960s to the 1980s focused on regulatory harmonization across member states, typically connected to the importance that EU bodies and member states placed on developing the single market. More recently, EU environmental policymaking has grappled with challenges of effective policy implementation and the integration of environmental and sustainability goals into other areas of policy. Building on previous discussions about EU actors and processes of agenda setting, policy-making, and implementation, this chapter examines nine major cases of EU environmental governance: air policy, water policy, waste management, chemicals management, GMOs, the CAP, the CFP, biodiversity, and climate change and renewable energy. Space does not permit the chapter to list and discuss all policy instruments in each area. Rather, short case studies highlight major policies and important dynamics to exemplify aspects of the increasingly multifaceted nature of EU environmental governance, including both policy accomplishments and shortcomings.

Air policy

Air pollution policy was among the first areas of European environmental law in the 1970s. Air pollutants, many travelling across national borders, have adverse environmental impacts on fresh water, soil, crops, and ecosystems. Pollutants also have negative human health effects, contributing to asthma and other respiratory problems, cardiovascular diseases, lung cancer. They are estimated to be the number one environmental cause of premature death in the EU. Pollutants furthermore damage physical materials and buildings, including those of cultural and historical importance. All these problems result in substantial direct costs and economic losses. A major trend over the past few decades is the movement away from air policies focused on narrow case-specific issues toward the formulation of more wide-ranging approaches. Most recently, the European Commission (in 2013) put forward a comprehensive Clean Air Policy Package, building on a 2005 Thematic Strategy on Air Pollution, toward fulfilling the goal of the seventh EAP of achieving "levels of air quality that do not give rise to significant negative impacts on, and risks to, human health and the environment."[1] In 2014 the package's components remained under consideration by the Council of the European Union and the European Parliament.

Air pollution law includes a large set of policy instruments, many updated on several occasions. These can be grouped into three core areas of air policy: 1) setting air quality standards, 2) mandating national emission reductions, and 3) regulating specific sources and sectors.[2] The first group of policies sets air quality standards by imposing target values (objectives on individual pollutants that should be met where possible) and limit values (thresholds for individual pollutants that should not be exceeded once attained) for ambient concentrations of specific air pollutants most harmful to human health. A 2004 directive covers arsenic, cadmium, mercury, nickel, and PAHs (polycyclic aromatic hydrocarbons) and a 2008 directive addresses sulfur dioxide, nitrogen oxides, carbon monoxide, benzene, particulate matter (PM10 and PM2.5), lead, and ozone. Under both directives, member states must divide their territories into smaller areas, continuously monitor ambient levels of all regulated pollutants in each of these, and implement measures to ensure compliance with set concentration thresholds. Most target and limit values entered into force in the 2005–12 period, but some PM2.5 standards have 2015 and 2020 deadlines.

The second group of emission reduction policies mandates national targets for separate pollutants to abate acidification, eutrophication, and ground-level ozone, largely leaving it to each member state to decide on specific implementing measures on top of EU laws for specific source categories. A 2001 directive set National Emission Ceilings (NECs) on maximum allowed emissions of sulfur dioxide, nitrogen oxide, VOCs (volatile organic compounds), and ammonia. A 1999 protocol to the 1979 Convention on Long-range Transboundary Air Pollution (CLRTAP, a regional treaty to which the EU and individual member states are parties) set similar ceilings, as well as standards for PM emissions, to have been attained by 2010.[3] As part of the 2013 Air Policy Package, the European Commission proposed a revised NEC directive with national caps for six air pollutants—the same five covered by the 2001 NEC directive and the 1999 CLRTAP protocol plus methane—with 2020 and 2030 deadlines. This proposal again intersects with CLRTAP and the adoption of a revised protocol in 2012 covering the same substances except methane, with 2020 target dates.

Differentiated NECs are set based on the concepts of critical loads (for acidification and eutrophication) and critical levels (for ground-level ozone).[4] Putting a focus on ecological effects of pollution, critical loads/levels are defined as the maximum amount of pollutants that ecosystems can withstand without being damaged. Related policy, where a country's contribution to the exceeding of critical loads/levels influences its emission reduction targets, is formulated based on modeling and measurements linking emission sources, transport patterns, depositions and effects, as finely gridded maps are used to track local-level ecological conditions and changes. The development of critical loads/levels, starting in the 1980s, was supported and pushed by the European Commission, the Scandinavian states, the Netherlands, and

Germany, contributing significant amounts of human and financial resources. The critical loads/levels approach remains central in setting tighter emission caps for individual substances and countries, towards the goal of not exceeding these anywhere in Europe.

The third group of air policies regulates emissions from specific sources or sectors by setting emission standards or imposing fuel mandates. These include a 2010 directive on integrated pollution prevention and control covering large stationary sources (including energy, metals, minerals, and chemical industries, waste facilities, and livestock farming), 2008 and 2009 regulations on vehicle emissions, 1994 and 1999 directives on VOC emissions from petrol and organic solvents, and several directives on fuel content. In addition, in 2013 the European Commission proposed a new directive on medium-sized combustion installations (e.g. smaller energy plants and industries). On many of these policies, the European Parliament and leader states had significant influence, competing over the design and stringency of specific mandates. For example, negotiations in the 1980s pitted German desires for uniform standards based on best available technologies against UK preferences of more discretion in implementing measures.[5] Many recent EU source-based policies apply such a technologically focused approach, often regarded as more expensive but easier to implement, monitor and enforce.

Looking forward, many people still breathe air that does not meet EU quality standards, and research shows that many pollutants are harmful at lower levels that previously believed. There have been notable reductions in ambient concentrations of sulfur dioxide, benzene, carbon monoxide, and lead, in some cases below policy goals, but other major pollutants—especially PM and ozone but also PAHs and nitrogen—pose a "significant threat" to human health, especially in urban areas where a majority of Europeans live.[6] On implementation, in 2011 Austria, Belgium, Finland, France, Germany, Ireland, Luxembourg, and Spain missed one or more NECs for the four pollutants with 2010 deadlines.[7] Industry, road transport, power plants, households, and agriculture all continue to emit substantial amounts of air pollution, as scientific assessments show that critical loads/levels are exceeded in many parts of Europe. Consequently, national emission mandates for the six pollutants identified by the European Commission in its proposed NEC directive revision will need to be revisited. In addition, transboundary transport of pollutants creates strong incentives for EU bodies and member states to continue their active engagement in regional and global multilateral forums dealing with air pollution.

Water policy

EU water law, like air legislation, dates to the 1970s and has grown substantially in 40 years. In the first three decades, a series of policy instruments yielded mixed results (at best).[8] In response, one of the largest and most ambitious pieces of environmental law in Europe was adopted in 2000: the Water Framework Directive (WFD). The general objective of the WFD is to achieve "good status" of all water within the EU by 2015, covering both surface water (e.g. lakes, rivers, transition waters, and coastal waters) and ground water. For surface water, good status refers to a combination of ecological status (the quality of the structure and functioning of aquatic ecosystems) and chemical status (pollutant-related quality standards, not be exceeded). For ground water, good status is measured in terms of chemical status (zero pollution and no effects on conductivity, a common indicator of pollution) and quantitative status (available water should not be exceeded by withdrawals over time). Toward these goals, the WFD is supplemented by separate legislation on drinking water, bathing water, urban waste water, and water pollution—each piece subject to substantial debate and prolonged negotiations between EU bodies, member states, and advocacy groups.

The WFD, the product of several years of contentious politics, introduced a more unified approach to water management. It is an enormous and demanding section of environmental law. Implementation is planned over 27 years, with many important decisions left to the discretion of member states. During the first nine years (2000–09) the WFD replaced several pieces of earlier legislation and introduced essential mandates. The subsequent 18-year implementation process is divided into three six-year management cycles (2009–15; 2015–21; and 2021–27). Importantly, the WFD mandates a fundamental reorganization of water management, seeking to address frequent mismatches between national and local political and administrative structures, and cross-cutting and often transnational hydrological systems. The WFD, shaped by the principle of integrated water resources management, focuses on catchment areas: the drainage area of rainwater heading for a common terminus. It establishes river basins as the main locus for water governance, rather than national or sub-national political jurisdictions.

Under the WFD, the EU divided river basins and associated coastal areas into 110 River Basin Districts. Forty of these are transnational, like the Danube and the Rhine river basins, covering roughly 60 percent of the EU.[9] Member states were mandated to formulate river basin management plans for each basin by 2009. These management plans, key tools for WFD implementation, required member states to establish administrative structures, conduct pressures and impact analyses and identify ecological baselines, create environmental monitoring and assessment programs, set management objectives, and design programs for implementation—all focused on river basins. For these processes and future management, the European Commission stresses the value of stakeholder consultation for meeting mandates on public participation and for engendering transparency to help ensure member states meet their obligations. Thus, the WFD is a pre-eminent example of a shift of authority away from the nation state; scientific research, environmental activism and policy expertise, and the subsidiarity principle all support the conclusion that water is often best governed at the river basin scale.[10]

The WFD's focus on water quality is based on the ecological effects of pollution and other stressors, similar to the critical loads/levels approach focus on ecological effects in air pollution policy. Under the WFD, member states designate their surface water bodies into one of three categories: natural, heavily modified (where human activity has substantially changed its character), or artificial (entirely created by humans). Only natural bodies are subject to the general good status goal. For the other two categories merely achieving lower protection targets of "good ecological potential" and "good chemical status" is required, because of hydromorphological pressures that cannot be removed due to high social or economic costs.[11] The WFD outlines natural, economic, and technical conditions that, if met for a specific water body, allow member states to extend the 2015 status deadlines up to 2027. A 2009 directive on setting environmental quality standards identifies 33 priority substances that, with nitrates, are of particular concern to the aquatic environment. In 2012, the European Commission proposed that 15 more substances be added to the priority list. Often substances of concern enter EU waters from outside sources, creating needs for cooperation through external forums.

The WFD also addresses water quantity issues. Related to a growing interest in financial instruments in environmental policy, the WFD requires that member states develop water policy based on the principle of full cost recovery (including environmental and resource costs). Applying the polluter pays principle, member states were required to introduce transparent water pricing that reflects "true costs" no later than 2010, to establish economic incentives for more efficient and sustainable water use. Additionally, the European Commission recently proposed that member states may voluntarily set up water allowance trading systems, where water access rights are bought and sold in an open market.[12] Such systems are viewed as most promising at the river basin level, rather than as a single EU-wide system like that used for some GHG emissions. In addition, a 2009 directive on eco-design supports the development of more water-efficient consumer goods and products, as EU policy seeks to reduce water demand and increase water efficiency also from this direction.

Looking forward, many Europeans enjoy clean tap water, can safely swim in many seas, lakes, and rivers, and can eat locally caught fish because pollution from industrial and urban sources is often well controlled. Yet, the 2015 good status goal was missed for almost half of all EU waters.[13] Also, significant differences in member state policy efforts and environmental records can be seen in Court of Justice rulings against Belgium, Greece, Portugal and Spain for not adopting river basin management plans, illustrating lagging and uneven implementation.[14] Large national variation exists in how many water bodies are classified as natural versus heavily modified or artificial, which has direct implications for the level of protection required, as well as the number of decisions seeking exemption from the 2015 deadlines.[15] Many governance structures are incomplete, including for efficient water pricing, and much management suffers from data shortages making it difficult to establish ecological baselines against which to measure progress.[16] Greater investment in WFD implementation and expanded international cooperation are necessary if EU water management goals are to be achieved.

Waste management

As EU member states grow wealthier, higher consumption levels result in the generation of more waste. Collectively, they produce 3 billion tonnes of waste each year, or 6 tonnes per person.[17] The 2008 Waste Framework Directive stipulates that all wastes must be handled without endangering human health or harming the environment, obligating member states to operate waste management plans and prevention programs. It stresses the importance of the polluter pays principle and extended producer responsibility, which shifts greater management responsibility onto firms. A 2000 directive establishes a classification system for hazardous and non-hazardous wastes. A 2006 directive details when wastes can be shipped between countries and bans export to developing countries, consistent with the global 1989 Basel convention on the transboundary transport of hazardous wastes.[18] In addition, over 20 directives and decisions exist on specific waste streams; waste management operations such as landfills, incineration, and port reception; national reporting on waste management; and connected issues such as urban waste-water treatment, ground water protection, and environmental impact assessments.[19]

Based on the concept of waste hierarchy, policy options are classified from "best" to "worst" from an environmental perspective:

1   Waste prevention—reduce waste levels as well as hazardousness by limiting the presence of dangerous substances in products.
2   Recycle and reuse—as many materials as possible should be recovered, preferably by recycling.
3   Improve final disposal and monitoring—wastes that cannot be recycled or reused should be safely incinerated with the use of landfill as a last resort.

Current legislation sets several 2020 targets: 70 percent of construction and demolition waste should be reused, recycled, or recovered; 50 percent of major kinds of household materials should be reused or recycled; and only 35 percent of the total amount of biodegradable municipal waste sent to landfill in 1995 should still go there. These targets are driven by a desire to make EU waste management more environmentally friendly and the fact that member states with high population density and active local communities are running out of new landfill options.

The first waste management law was introduced in 1975, starting a long process of tensions between EU efforts to create uniform standards and member states' diverging policy styles, interests, and management capabilities—sometimes related to debates over the application of the subsidiarity principle. Since then, several broad directives give member states considerable flexibility in taking regulatory measures. Consistent with experiences in other federal and multilevel systems, this resulted in a large variety of national implementation measures, ranging from mandatory taxes, recycling schemes, and deposit systems to voluntary agreements with industry. Much early waste law was driven by national initiatives prompting EU action, rather than by EU bodies taking leadership roles. Early on, market issues often trumped environmental concerns, but an important 1988 ruling by the Court of Justice allowed Denmark to operate a restrictive bottle recycling scheme.[20] This decision helped to expand the room for environmental action, as Denmark together with Germany and the Netherlands took on environmental leadership roles in designing more environmentally ambitious waste laws after the SEA.

Since the 1980s, efforts to raise national mandates and protection measures have involved contentious debates about binding versus voluntary waste targets, levels of appropriate ambition, and how far member states can go in setting their own standards.[21] The formulation of the 1994 directive on packaging and packaging waste illustrated all of these issues, as the European Commission, the Council of the European Union, and the European Parliament competed for influence. Its adoption was related to a 1991 German packaging ordinance seen by other member states as protectionist and infringing on free trade. The German ordinance shifted responsibility to industry for handling waste, but with unintended consequences. Higher German private sector costs led to increased waste exports, impacting prices and management systems in other member states. It also resulted in illegal waste dumping, mainly in Eastern Europe. These effects demonstrate the ongoing complexity of governing interconnected trade and environment issues.

More recently, growing concerns about electronic waste ("e-waste") are driving continued action by leader states in collaboration with the European Commission and the European Parliament. The 2012 directive on waste electrical and electronic equipment (WEEE), updating the original 2002 version, regulates 10 common categories of electrical and electronic equipment, intending to increase recovery and recycling to reduce amounts going to final disposal.[22] Through industry responsibility, consumers return used goods to producers for recycling, reprocessing, and safe disposal. This is intended to provide market-based incentives to design more environmentally friendly electrical and electronic goods. Furthermore, the 2011 directive on the restriction of the use of certain hazardous substances in electrical and electronic equipment (RoHS), initially passed in 2002, limits the use of six hazardous substances in the WEEE directive's 10 product categories, as well as all other types of electrical and electronic equipment, to reduce the risk that such substances are released into the environment, causing water pollution and human health problems.[23]

Looking forward, EU laws and related waste hierarchy initiatives have succeeded in reducing the amount of waste going to landfill, but they have not sufficiently decoupled waste generation from economic growth, a critical issue identified in the Sustainable Development Strategy.[24] Large national differences in waste generation and waste management capabilities remain, yielding substantial implementation deficits on key pieces of legislation.[25] As a result, waste policy is among those areas subject to the highest number of European Commission infringement procedures against member states. It seems unlikely that 2020 policy goals on reuse and recycling will be met. Yet, EU actions to phase out hazardous substances in electrical and electronic goods, and expanding private sector responsibilities for their handling after final disposal, have fundamentally changed practices in Europe and around the world.[26] These policy efforts have important connections to hazardous chemicals management.

Chemicals management

EU chemicals law is structured around the large and complex 2007 regulation on the registration, evaluation, authorisation and restriction of chemicals (REACH) and the 2009 regulation on the classification, labelling and packaging of substances and mixtures (CLP). Specific categories of chemicals, including biocides and pesticides, are covered by separate legislation. Many of these laws are connected to commitments under regional and global treaties.[27] The first directive on hazardous substances dates to 1967, primarily aiming to harmonize controls across member states to facilitate trade within the single market. Controls based on more direct environmental and health concerns were strengthened several times. In the 2000s, years of political debate culminated in the REACH regulation, pioneered by a coalition of green leader states (e.g. Sweden, Denmark, the Netherlands, Germany, Austria, and the UK), DG Environment, MEPs, and environmental advocacy groups in the face of considerable industry opposition.[28] The regulation was intended to create a more comprehensive, proactive and faster system for managing chemical risks in industrial processes and finished goods.

The REACH regulation replaced several earlier laws and is scheduled to be fully implemented in 2018. Impacting most firms across the EU and EFTA—as well as many outside the EU—its adoption pursues a goal in the first Sustainable Development Strategy, to "by 2020, ensure that chemicals are only produced and used in ways that do not pose significant threats to human health and the environment." The REACH regulation is also consistent with priorities outlined in the sixth EAP, including generating more policy-relevant risk assessment data, expanding risk management and earlier identification of dangerous chemicals based on their intrinsic properties connected to the precautionary principle, and accelerating substitution of toxic chemicals with safer ones or alternative technologies. It is designed to ensure free movement of chemicals on the single market, shifting responsibilities for chemicals management from public authorities to industry. Chemicals management continues to include many spirited debates among

EU bodies, member states, and stakeholder groups over how best to operationalize precautionary measures.[29]

Initially, industry had to pre-register chemicals produced or used in quantities of over 1 tonne per year by 2008, generating a list of 143,000 chemicals involving 65,000 firms.[30] During the registration process firms submit a technical dossier to the ECHA on the properties and uses of chemicals they manufacture or import, as well as an assessment of the hazards and potential risks they present and how these may be controlled. Registration deadlines depend on substances' inherent properties and the quantities in which they are manufactured or imported. For carcinogenic, mutagenic, or toxic to reproduction substances above 1 tonne per year, substances dangerous to aquatic organisms or the environment above 100 tonnes per year, and others manufactured or imported at 1,000 tonnes or more per year there was a 2010 deadline (resulting in over 24,500 dossiers covering 4,300 substances). For those manufactured or imported at 100–1,000 tonnes per year, the deadline was 2013, gathering over 9,000 dossiers covering 3,000 substances. For those manufactured or imported at 1–100 tonnes per year, the deadline is 2018. The emerging result is a truly massive amount of information about chemical risks and management practices.

Member states and the ECHA, which plays a central role in implementation, divide registered substances into three categories for evaluation. The first of these seeks to identify "substances of very high concern," where all use is banned after a certain date if not explicitly authorized by the European Commission. Authorizations, time-limited and subject to re-review, are given if risks are adequately controlled, socioeconomic benefits outweigh risks, or there are no alternatives. The second category lists substances for restriction. Any member state, or the ECHA at the request of the European Commission, may propose restrictions. These proposals are open to external comments from industry, environmental groups, and other stakeholders. If the evaluation shows risks needing to be addressed, the European Commission may propose restrictions on all or specific uses to be considered by member states under the comitology system's examination procedure. The third category contains hazardous substances targeted for harmonized classification and labeling (e.g. the use of standardized symbols, phrases, and packaging conditions) to inform users and building from the CLP regulation.

A five-year European Commission-led review of the REACH regulation concluded that it was too early to quantify environmental and human health benefits, but noted progress in addressing chemical risks.[31] The initial registration system brought both quantitative and qualitative improvements in assessment data. Increased substance-specific information resulted in classification changes, with most having become more stringent. Improved safety data sheets for communication down supply chains (supplier to customer) and upstream on new hazard information (customer to supplier) have resulted in additional risk management measures. Increased controls on substances of very high concern have triggered accelerated substitution. However, the review also noted problems with incomplete registration dossiers, insufficient assessments of particular substances, inadequate information on some safety data sheets, and high administrative burdens and financial costs, particularly for small and medium-sized enterprises related to compiling technical dossiers and paying registration fees.

Looking forward, the scope of the REACH regulation is both a major strength and a source of concern regarding how well implemented it will be by 2018. Putting the REACH regulation into practice demonstrates the significance of the comitology procedure and how politically important post-adoption clarifying of obligations and standards, including by ECHA, can be. This process creates multiple opportunities for leader states and environmental groups to influence rule making, and registration and authorization decisions. These interrelated scientific, technical, and political processes are critical to operationalize the precautionary principle into risk assessment and management. In addition, industry actors and some member states express concerns over administrative and financial issues and how the REACH regulation may impact European firm competitiveness in globalized markets. There is also a need to continue assessing how the implementation of the REACH and CLP regulations affect other policies to minimize regulatory and bureaucratic redundancies and contradictions. Lastly, similar to waste management, a big question remains open: Can economic growth be decoupled from continuous use of hazardous substances?

Genetically modified organisms (GMOs)

GMO policy remains highly controversial in Europe. A GMO is a plant, animal or micro-organism (such as bacteria or fungi) whose genetic material has been technically altered to yield a new property—for example, resistance to disease or insects or improvement of nutritional value—using recombinant DNA technology rather than natural cross-breeding. GMOs fall under the auspices of DG Health and Consumers, as they raise a number of sustainable development issues related to biodiversity, human health, consumer rights, agricultural production, and international trade. GMO policymaking regularly involves clashes between EU bodies, member states, industry organizations, farmers, environmental advocacy groups, and consumers over appropriate structures and principles for risk assessment, control, and communication.[32] Current EU law, intended to strike a balance between highly divergent opinions based on both deeply held values and significant material interests, consists of several policy instruments on the introduction and handling of GMOs.

A 2001 directive on the deliberate release into the environment of GMOs establishes a methodology for assessing environmental risks and approving intentional release and placing on the market of GMOs. A connected 2003 regulation on genetically modified food and feed creates an authorization process for three types of products: 1) GMOs for food and feed use; 2) food and feed containing GMOs; and 3) food and feed produced from or containing ingredients produced from GMOs. A second, complementary 2003 regulation on the traceability and labeling of GMOs and the traceability of food and feed products produced from GMOs mandates a compulsory labeling scheme to inform consumers and give them the ability to choose between GMO products or non-GMO items in their local stores. A third 2003 regulation sets up a system for notifying and exchanging information on transboundary movements of GMOs to countries outside the EU, consistent with commitments under the 2000 Cartagena Protocol on Biosafety to the global 1992 Convention on Biological Diversity.

Like other early GMO adopters, initial EU policy in the 1990s was based on the principle of substantial equivalence: if a new GMO food or food component was found to be the same as (e.g. substantially equivalent to) an old food or food component, it could be treated in the same manner with respect to safety regulation. As European GMO opposition grew, Austria in 1997 and Luxembourg in 1998 invoked a "safeguard clause" in early legislation, imposing domestic bans on the use and/or sale of specific EU-approved GMOs, based on human health or environmental concerns. In 1998, a deeply divided Council of the European Union was unable to agree on a request by the European Commission to repeal these bans. In 1999, the Council of the European Union agreed on a de facto (but not legally binding) moratorium on new GMO authorizations until new legislation was in place (as additional member states invoked the safeguard clause). The resultant laws, still in effect, replaced the principle of substantial equivalence with the precautionary principle and introduced stricter rules for assessment, approval, and tracing.[33]

The current GMO authorization system is outlined in the 2001 directive on intentional environmental releases of GMOs (for cultivation) and the 2003 regulation on GM food and feed (for placing products on the single market). The process starts with the submission of a GMO authorization application by a firm to any member state. This application is followed by a risk assessment of environmental and human health issues, where EFSA fulfills central tasks in collaboration with member state national agencies. Once completed, the risk assessment is submitted to the European Commission, which drafts a decision for or against authorization, taking into account the precautionary principle. This draft decision is then considered and voted on by member states under the examination procedure, according to the current comitology structure. While member states and most stakeholders voice broad support for the overall policy objectives and principles of this authorization system, many express concerns about long application processes and the functioning of the single market, especially with respect to the "dysfunctional" system for assessing applications for cultivation.[34]

The de facto moratorium on GMO authorizations was lifted in 2004, with the approval of a maize variety (Syngenta's Bt11). In 2013, over 50 GMOs were approved and registered for import.[35] While GMOs in food remain relatively rare in Europe, they increasingly dominate in feed (in both cases subject to labeling).[36] In contrast, the system for reviewing cultivation applications remains effectively frozen, due to political disagreement between member states, shaped by domestic politics. In 2012, only MON810 (an insect-resistant maize owned by Monsanto and authorized in 1998) was grown commercially for feed on roughly 100,000 hectares, mainly in Spain. In comparison, about 100 GMO varieties were approved globally, grown over 170 million hectares in 28 countries that same year.[37] Another GMO—Amflora, a genetically optimized starch potato—was authorized in 2010 but voluntarily withdrawn by the owner BASF in 2012 due to public opposition. Furthermore, the General Court overturned this approval in 2013, citing a failure by the European Commission to fulfill its procedural obligations.[38] In 2013 the European Commission proposed that member states, for only the third time, approve a new GMO for cultivation (an insect-resistant maize developed by DuPont and Dow Chemical).

Looking forward, several member states, including Austria, France, Greece, Hungary, Germany and Luxembourg, continue to prohibit the use and/or sale of EU-approved GMOs, with strong support from environmental groups and domestic public opinion. Attempting to break the political gridlock, the European Commission in 2010 proposed that each member state be given the authority to make its own GMO cultivation decisions, but by early 2014 member states had failed to reach an agreement. Nevertheless, the European Commission, with support from countries such as Spain, Sweden and the UK and the multinational biotechnology and agriculture industry, pushes for more flexibility and acceptance of GMO cultivation and food. In addition, the EU is under considerable pressure from the United States and other countries where GMOs are commonly grown—and the World Trade Organization (WTO)—to relax its mandates. As such, EU GMO policy continues to attract substantial attention in Europe and internationally, as strongly held policy positions remain far apart.[39] It also illustrates the difficulty of achieving policy consensus on issues where there are deep-seated differences on basic values and principles.

The Common Agricultural Policy (CAP)

The CAP has long been politically, economically and environmentally contentious in Europe and beyond; all the more so in recent years, as agriculture is essential to sustainable development. Environmentally, agricultural policy overlaps with other major issues such as biodiversity protection, water quality, regulations on fertilizer and pesticide use, GMO controls, and animal protection. Socially, agricultural issues intersect with efforts to support rural areas and farming communities and maintain consumer confidence in food quality and safety. Economically, agriculture and rural development constitute over 40 percent of the EU budget, with additional funds allocated through national budgets. Member states recently receiving the most annual CAP payments include France (17 percent), Spain (13 percent), Germany (12 percent), Italy (11 percent), and the UK (7 percent).[40] Membership enlargements since 2004 have doubled the number of EU farmers to approximately 14 million, as agriculture and the agri-foods industry account for 6 percent of the EU GDP.[41] Yet farmers operate under varying conditions, as 20 percent of "farmers" are large agri-businesses and big landowners which receive 80 percent of the EU aid.[42]

The CAP, which came into effect in 1962, includes all 28 member states, but not the EFTA countries. It has been subject to several revisions, changing both overall objectives and the use of specific policy mechanisms. The most recent reform package, the result of extensive multi-year negotiations among the European Commission, the Council of the European Union, and the European Parliament, passed in 2013. It focused on three sets of priorities: 1) viable food production; 2) sustainable management of natural resources; and 3) balanced development of rural areas throughout the EU.[43] While there is substantial European official and public support for these broad priorities, their fulfillment involves a multitude of policies and programs around which exists substantial disagreement among member states and extensive lobbying by farmer, environmental, and industry organizations. Much controversy concerns the amount of money allocated in the EU budget to the CAP and rural development, and how this money is spent (in 2013, €57.5 billion, or €0.30 per person per day).

The Rome Treaty's inclusion of agriculture in Article 38 was based on a carefully crafted compromise, mainly between France and Germany. France insisted on the CAP to protect its farmers as a prerequisite for accepting the free movement of industrial goods, a key objective for Germany. Initially, it was designed to increase agricultural productivity and make member states more self-sustaining. The CAP not only provided production subsidies, where farmers got more money the more they produced, but also offered a price guarantee—the EEC intervened in the market and bought agricultural products if they fell below a set price. The EEC taxed imports and, starting in the 1970s, subsidized exports of agricultural products. Collectively, this had three major results: 1) the EEC went from a situation of food shortages to major "food mountains"—producing more than the regional demand; 2) surplus, cheap products were sold on international markets, making it difficult for farmers elsewhere, including in developing countries, to compete; and 3) European food prices remained high, affecting everyday consumers in all member states.

Soaring CAP costs—to over 70 percent of the EU budget in the 1980s—eventually triggered reforms. These initially addressed over-production (food mountains peaked in the 1980s) and reduced expenditures by gradually stopping subsidies based on the volume of production and scaling back export subsidies.[44] Related to the 2014–20 multiannual financial framework, the 2013 CAP reform progressively reduces differences in income support to farmers in different countries to make the CAP more economically fair to newer member states. Previously, the 15 countries that were members before 2004 received higher levels of financial support. The 2013 reform also continues an effort to "green" the CAP (and thereby the EU budget). Fewer resources will go toward basic income support in favor of practices that benefit, for example, biodiversity protection and climate change goals. Similarly, recent reforms stress the importance of measures to help farmers in the context of rural development, and a small portion of CAP funds (less than 10 percent) constitute market support, for example when bad weather impacts farming and produce markets.

While France, Greece, Poland and other member states and large agri-business groups that benefit from the CAP resist change, critics, including Sweden, the UK, Denmark, the Netherlands and Germany, argue that reforms have not gone far enough to reduce expenditures, liberalize markets, and support environmental objectives. In 2007 Sweden was the first member state to propose phasing out all subsidies for export, intervention, and production, leaving only subsidies for environmental protection.[45] Food safety and animal health issues are also tangled up in agricultural policy. In the wake of several food scandals (including "mad cow" disease), consumers demanded higher production standards and better health protection by national agencies and EU bodies including EFSA.[46] There is also growing interest in organic farming, rooted in a social movement opposing large-scale "industrial" faming.[47] EU policy in this area includes the 2007 regulation on organic production and labeling of organic products, which excludes GMOs from qualifying for organic labeling. Interestingly, despite significant transatlantic differences over agricultural subsidies and GMOs, US and EU organic standards show substantial convergence in recent years.[48]

Looking forward, the CAP is linked to EU initiatives to enhance the competitiveness of farmers and the food industry related to the Europe 2020 Strategy and the Sustainable Development Strategy. To assess progress, the European Commission plans another CAP report in 2018. Around the same time, the need to determine the next multi-annual financial framework for beyond 2020 will force another round of budget negotiations. As some member states remain fiercely protective of the financial benefits their farmers receive under the CAP, and direct payments constitute 30 percent of agricultural incomes on average at the Union level, the EU remains a long way from Sweden's proposal to abolish all subsidies not aimed at environmental protection. Nevertheless a growing number of member states question the overall size of the CAP budget.[49] In addition, EU bodies and member states struggle to achieve deeper integration of environmental and animal welfare concerns into CAP's financial dimensions and on-the-ground farming practices. Such greater integration will be necessary to meet several critical environmental and sustainable development goals.

The Common Fisheries Policy (CFP)

EU fisheries policy is another highly contentious, long-standing natural resource and sustainable development issue. Most European commercially traded fish stocks are in decline with many critically threatened. The EU-wide fishing fleet consists of over 83,000 vessels, with over 75 percent of these registered in Greece, Spain, Italy, Portugal, France, and the UK.[50] The total fleet has declined by over 23,000 boats since

1995, but estimates suggest that it is still two to three times larger than available fish stocks can support, while technological development further improves the ability to locate and catch fish and extends the amount of time boats can stay at sea.[51] The member states responsible for the largest catches are Denmark (15 percent), Spain (15 percent), and the UK (12 percent). The EU seafood processing industry—which has an annual value of €20 billion and employs 120,000 people across 3,700 firms—is dominated by Spain (19 percent), the United Kingdom (15 percent), and France (13 percent). Spain (26 percent), Poland (17 percent), and Italy (10 percent) were the largest recipients of EU fisheries aid during the 2007–13 period.[52]

The CFP, the central policy instrument for fisheries and aquaculture management, was first launched in 1983. Like the CAP, the CFP does not extend to any countries outside the EU. The CFP was revised many times over 30 years, most recently in 2013. Rhetorically, it seeks to make fishing environmentally, socially, and economically sustainable. The latest efforts to improve the CFP toward these goals, by the European Commission, the Council of the European Union, and the European Parliament, attempted to address the poor record of EU fisheries policy, cut subsidies supporting overcapacity, and reduce wasted fisheries products dumped at sea. During the revisions, many MEPs and environmental advocacy groups pushed member states toward more substantial, if still inadequate, conservation goals including greater funding for monitoring and research involving EFCA. These measures were taken against the backdrop that 30 percent of Europe's commercial fish stocks are fished beyond safe biological limits and 70 percent of commercial stocks were fished above maximum sustainable yield in 2010.[53]

The Rome Treaty included a direct reference to fishery issues in the agriculture section (Article 38), but little action was taken before the 1970s. For decades member states remained deeply divided over issues of fishing rights, trade liberalization, and efforts to transfer policy-making competence to the EU level. Conflicts between harmonization efforts and issues connected with national sovereignty, fishing rights, territorial waters, and the defense of local fishing communities remain common.[54] The first EEC measures set basic rules for access to fishing grounds, markets, and industry structures. EU fishers have equal access to member state waters, but coastal waters were reserved for locals who traditionally fish these areas. Adopted policies created a common market in fisheries products and supported modernization of fishing vessels and on-shore installations. In 1976, member states followed the international movement and extended their exclusive economic zones of rights to marine resources from 12 to 200 nautical miles.

The CFP was established to better account for environmental, economic, and social dimensions of fishing. It included four main areas of policymaking and standard setting: 1) conservation of fish stocks and setting of Total Allowable Catches (TACs); 2) regulations of structures (such as vessels, port facilities, and fish processing plants); 3) the single market for fish products; and 4) external fisheries policy, including agreements with non-EU members and negotiations in international organizations. National TACs were divided among member states on a yearly basis in the Council of the European Union, with the European Commission playing an important mediator role. A 1992 review showed that there were too many vessels and that technical measures alone could not prevent overfishing; total catches also had to be regulated. The 2002 review demonstrated that attempts to implement a comprehensive fisheries policy had failed, with many stocks declining since 1994. The situation continues to worsen, with many stock sizes and landings declining dramatically over the past 25 years.

In 2009, then Fisheries Commissioner Joe Borg spoke for many when he called the CFP a "disaster."[55] The fishing fleet had not been downsized to an appropriate capacity, scientific advice remained marginalized during policymaking, structural measures were often resisted by member states (such as mesh-size regulations), and many regulations were poorly enforced despite efforts by the EFCA.[56] Yet, fundamental change was resisted by member states with large fishing fleets and processing industries benefiting from the status quo—notably Spain and Portugal. Some member states with the support of national fisheries organizations, continue to seek the largest possible national quotas. Other member states, backed by environmental advocacy groups and scientists, push to limit quotas and the overall TACs—so far, largely in vain. Because scientific data suggest fish capture and industry capacity should be much lower than current levels, some member states also work to limit the authority of scientific and technical information and actors—an all-too-common tactic in fisheries politics around the world.

Looking forward, the 2013 CFP reform package reshaped some policies, but did little to create sustainable fisheries management. While the European Commission sets overall quotas, neither it nor EFCA has the capacity to monitor and enforce regulations on individual vessels, a task some member states take much more seriously than others. The translation of scientific data into the adoption of TACs and other policy measures remains slow and incomplete, as other national political, social and economic factors often take precedence. Furthermore, high EU consumer demand means that many marine resources are imported, mainly from Norway, China, Iceland, Vietnam, and

Morocco, contributing to overfishing in external waters. The EU also concluded access agreements, paying over US$300 million annually, with countries in West Africa and elsewhere to give member state boats fishing rights in other countries' exclusive economic zones—putting additional pressure on already fragile marine resources outside the Union.[57] Lastly, integrating with the CFP is a major obstacle for any possible future EU membership for Iceland and Norway.

Biodiversity protection

EU biodiversity policy—seeking to protect the large variety of ecosystems, species and genes existing across Europe—is another area where EU bodies, member states, and stakeholder groups struggle to make progress. The present Biodiversity Strategy, adopted by the European Commission in 2011, sets out a 2020 "headline target" and a 2050 "vision."[58] The short-term headline target, agreed to by the European Council in 2010, is "halting the loss of biodiversity and the degradation of ecosystem services in the EU by 2020, and restoring them in so far as feasible, while stepping up the EU contribution to averting global biodiversity loss." The longer-range vision is that by 2050 EU biodiversity and the ecosystem services it provides (its natural capital) should be "protected, valued and appropriately restored for biodiversity's intrinsic value and for their essential contribution to human well-being and economic prosperity, and so that catastrophic changes caused by the loss of biodiversity are avoided." Fulfilling these objectives requires reversing many ecological trends all over Europe.

Drivers of biodiversity loss in Europe include land use and habitat change, overexploitation of natural resources, pollution, the spread of invasive species, and ecological change induced by climate change. Even if it is notoriously difficult to "value" nature, Europe's continuing loss of biodiversity has enormous economic and social consequences.[59] Linked in part to commitments under the global biodiversity convention, EU policy seeks to protect biodiversity for different reasons, including benefits provided by direct use, bioremediation (natural organisms breaking down pollutants), organisms' contributions to medicine, and ecosystem services (such as water purification).[60] The Biodiversity Strategy was adopted in response to failure to meet an earlier target to halt the loss of biodiversity and restore habitats and natural systems by 2010. Currently, only 17 percent of habitats and species and 11 percent of key ecosystems covered by EU legislation are in a favorable state.[61] A majority of ecosystems are degraded to points that they no longer deliver valuable services.[62]

To help EU bodies and member states operationalize the Biodiversity Strategy, measure progress, and assess where additional measures are needed, the 2020 target is broken down into six more specific targets with their own indicators. The first target calls for full implementation of the two main pieces of EU conservation legislation—the 2009 directive on the conservation of wild birds (first adopted in 1979) and the 1992 directive on the conservation of natural habitats of wild fauna and flora—toward improved status of protected species and areas. The second target focuses on maintaining and improving restoration of ecosystems and the services they provide. The third target seeks to increase the contribution of agriculture and forestry to maintaining and enhancing biodiversity, and the fourth target aims to ensure the sustainable use of fisheries resources. The fifth target addresses the need to combat invasive alien species damaging ecosystems, while the sixth target stresses the importance of EU efforts in international politics to avert global biodiversity loss.

Key to the fulfillment of the Biodiversity Strategy is the completion of the Natura 2000 network, with far-reaching political and organizational implications for member states.[63] This initiative moves away from a narrow species-specific focus to an ecosystems-based approach, where member states are required to establish "special areas of conservation" under the 1992 habitats directive, "special protection areas" under the 2009 birds directive, and "marine protected areas" under the 2009 marine strategy framework directive. The whole network of these areas includes over 26,000 sites covering 18 percent of EU territory and 4 percent of European waters within the 200 nautical miles exclusive economic zone (additional marine areas are protected under other non-EU exclusive regional seas agreements).[64] Member states are responsible for designation and management of sites, but the EU provides co-financing. Protected areas not only include traditional nature reserves where economic activities are restricted, but also both public and private land, where the focus is on ensuring sustainable natural resources use.

The Biodiversity Strategy's 2020 targets on agriculture, forestry and fisheries highlight how dependent successful biodiversity protection is on integration of biodiversity concerns into other policy areas. The CFP and the CAP, including rural development policy, have significant implications for ecosystems and species value and how natural resources are managed across regional, national, and local levels. Even if biodiversity, agriculture, forestry and fisheries are typically treated as separate issues during policymaking and implementation, their de facto connections illustrate the importance of improved policy integration towards better environmental protection and sustainable development.

The same is true for biodiversity policy's connections to GMO standards and climate change action, including biofuels mandates. Lastly, 2020 targets five and six on invasive species and international cooperation bring attention to the inherently transnational aspects of biodiversity management—EU policy decisions are taken in the context of global biodiversity and climate change crises.[65]

Looking forward, the EU has clearly failed to reverse negative biodiversity trends. The Natura 2000 network has positive effects in individual member states, but collectively these are insufficient to limit damaging activities significantly. The European Commission receives many complaints from nongovernmental groups about member states' failure to design and manage protected areas properly. Large differences remain in the management of protected areas across Europe, including around the involvement of stakeholders and local communities. The European public remains generally unaware of the Natura 2000 network and significant variation exists in public awareness and concern about biodiversity—and the extent to which individuals feel personally affected by biodiversity loss.[66] Even if the connection between public opinion and successful policy implementation remains unclear, raising public consciousness about the importance of biodiversity issues continues to be an important dimension of improving European biodiversity governance.

Climate change and renewable energy

Climate change is a high-profile issue in the EU, evidenced by the creation of DG Climate Action. Consistent with the precautionary principle, the EU leads support for the goal that global average surface temperatures should not increase by more than 2°C above pre-industrial levels. To meet that goal, global GHG emissions would have to peak around 2020 and then fall dramatically (around −80 percent) by 2050. A host of EU goals and policies are connected to global climate change politics and institutions, including under the 1992 United Nations Framework Convention on Climate Change (UNFCCC) and the 1997 Kyoto Protocol. Political struggles among EU bodies and differences in member states' ambitions and interests greatly impact climate and energy policymaking. Slightly over 11 percent of global GHG emissions originate in the EU. European per capita emissions are higher than those of most developing countries, but some member states compare well. In 2010, for example, Romania's 3.7 tonnes and Sweden's 5.6 tonnes of CO_2 emissions per person were lower than China's 6.2 tonnes, Australia's 16.9 tonnes, and the United States' 17.6 tonnes per person.[67]

The 2009 Climate and Energy Package sets out three main "20-20-20" goals for 2020: 1) cutting GHG emissions by 20 percent below 1990 levels; 2) improving energy efficiency by 20 percent compared with a 2007 reference projection for 2020; and 3) increasing the total share of renewable energy consumption to 20 percent. A 2014 agreement set additional goals for 2030: a 40 percent reduction in GHGs, 27 percent energy consumption coming from renewable sources, and a 27 percent energy saving. On cutting GHG emissions, effort sharing features prominently. To fulfill an early EU commitment of an 8 percent reduction in GHG emissions from 1990 levels by 2012 under the Kyoto Protocol, wealthier countries such as Denmark and Germany agreed to cut their emissions more (both by 21 percent), so that less affluent ones could increase theirs (Portugal by 27 percent and Greece by 25 percent). To reduce GHG emissions from sectors not covered by the ETS by 10 percent below 2005 levels by 2020 (such as transport, buildings, agriculture and waste), national targets again partly reflect member states' relative wealth. They range from 20 percent reductions for Denmark, Ireland, and Luxembourg, to a 20 percent increase for Bulgaria. National renewable energy targets for 2020, based on different starting points and short-term means to increase production, vary from 10 percent for Malta to 49 percent for Sweden.

The European Commission issued the first strategy to limit CO2 emissions and improve energy efficiency in 1991.[68] Policy efforts in the mid-1990s attempted to find a way for the then 15 member states to meet the collective target of 8 percent GHG reduction below 1990 levels by 2012. These included a failed European Commission-led initiative to create an EU-wide carbon tax, vetoed by the UK in the Council of the European Union (requiring consensus as a taxation issue). However, several member states have modest national carbon taxes. Since then, the EU has adopted a wide range of policy instruments that target choices and behavior by governments, firms, and individuals, designed to help meet the 2020 goals.[69] After the carbon tax proposal failed, EU bodies and member states turned their attention to another market-based policy instrument: emissions trading. Based on a 2003 directive, most recently amended in 2009, the ETS includes the EU plus Iceland, Lichtenstein, and Norway. It developed through three trading periods (2005–07, 2008–12, and 2013–20), with significant modifications and controversy over time.

The current (third) ETS period includes a regional cap on three GHGs (carbon dioxide, nitrous oxide, and perfluorocarbons) from more than 11,000 major point sources in power generation and manufacturing and aviation, covering 45 percent of all EU GHGs.[70] The cap shrinks annually so that emissions from covered sectors in 2020 will be 21 percent lower than in 2005. The European Commission allots allowances to each participating country which in turn allocates these to domestic firms where allowances are increasingly auctioned off (rather than handed out for free) across different sectors. Some preferential treatment is given to countries joining since 2004. Allowances may be traded and firms are fined if they do not have enough allowance to cover their emissions by the end of each calendar year. Firms can also use emission credits generated under the Kyoto Protocol. Beyond the ETS, the EU has set CO2 emission standards for cars and vans, as the transport sector is responsible for over 30 percent of EU GHG emissions. While GHG emissions in several sectors decreased 15 percent between 1990 and 2007, they increased 36 percent from transportation during the same period.

EU renewable energy policy attempts to reduce GHG emissions and dependency on imported energy. A 2009 directive outlining a framework for the production and promotion of energy from renewable sources is linked to implementation of varying national renewable energy targets for 2020, including achieving a 10 percent share of renewable energy in transportation. Member states have a high degree of freedom to decide in which renewable energy sources to invest (biomass, hydro, wind, etc.). Yet, they disagree greatly over the use of fossil fuels and alternative energy sources with entrenched and powerful national industry interests. This includes widely diverging attitudes towards emerging issues such as hydraulic fracturing for natural gas extraction and long-standing disagreements over nuclear power (see Box 5.1).[71] On energy efficiency, the 2009 directive on eco-design promotes the development of more energy-efficient products. Another 2009 directive establishes a framework of standards on the development and safe use of carbon capture and storage.

Box 5.1 Nuclear energy in the EU—no unity in diversity

Nuclear energy exemplifies the tremendous challenges the EU faces when member states and societies have fundamental disagreements on an issue. Some countries, like Austria and Denmark, never had commercial nuclear power plants in operation. Others, like Germany and Sweden, have taken decisions to phase out all existing nuclear plants, while another group of member states is heavily dependent on and invested in nuclear power and may expand it over time, including France, the Czech Republic, Finland, and the United Kingdom. As a result, EU nuclear energy policy consists largely of some basic safety, emergency response and public notification standards, with little regional discussion of the future scope of the nuclear industry in Europe.

Looking forward, data show a mixed picture.[72] EU-15 GHG emissions declined on average by 12.2 percent from 1990 to the 2008–12 period, exceeding the Kyoto Protocol target. Yet, Austria, Luxembourg, Italy, and Spain missed their targets and must acquire credits to make up the difference. The EU is on track to surpass its 2020 GHG reduction goal—EU-27 emissions were 18 percent below 1990 levels in 2012—but transportation emissions remain high. Also, Austria, Belgium, Finland, Ireland, Luxembourg, and Spain lack the necessary plans to meet their GHG targets. The EU will likely meet its 2020 renewable energy target, but only Bulgaria, Denmark, France, and Germany are making good progress towards their energy efficiency targets. The years 2012–14 were tough for climate change and renewable energy advocates. The EU encountered difficulties to strengthen policy goals for 2030 and beyond (with some EU bodies and advocates pushing more ambitious goals than those adopted in 2014), the ETS struggles to reduce GHG emissions effectively and efficiently, and costs of renewable energy investments have resulted in calls to delay action. Many EU efforts are also influenced by international politics and the slow (or absent) progress toward meaningful global climate change cooperation.

Increased standards and mixed outcomes

Taken together, the different environmental cases in this chapter demonstrate the enormous growth in the scope, stringency and level of ambition of EU environmental and sustainability policy goals, and the substantial variance in implementation and environmental outcomes. For all issue areas, with the possible exception of the CAP and the CFP, data suggest that environmental outcomes might well be worse absent years of EU policy and standard setting. In some areas of air, water, waste, chemicals, climate change and renewable energy policy, it is clear that EU initiatives have produced numerous positive environmental results. Yet, many of the overall European ecological trends remain negative and some policy areas—like the CAP, the CFP and biodiversity—are widely viewed as environmental failures. In addition, all of these environmental cases are embedded in global and transnational relations, where the EU both seeks to shape many international decisions and standards and can be greatly impacted by a multitude of external processes and pressures.

Notes

1 The European Parliament and the Council of the European Union, *General Union Environment Action Programme to 2020 "Living Well, Within the Limits of Our Planet"* (2013), para. 15.
2 European Environment Agency, *Air Quality in Europe—2013 Report* (Copenhagen, 2013).
3 Henrik Selin and Stacy D. VanDeveer, "Institutional Linkages and European Air Pollution Politics," in *Governing the Air: The Dynamics of Science, Policy and Citizen Interaction*, ed. R. Lidskog and G. Sundqvist (Cambridge, Mass.: MIT Press, 2011), 61–92.
4 Jørgen Wettestad, *Clearing the Air: European Advances in Tackling Acid Rain and Atmospheric Pollution* (Aldershot: Ashgate, 2002).
5 Sonja Boehmer-Christiansen and Jim Skea, *Acid Politics: Environmental and Energy Politics in Britain and Germany* (New York: Belhaven Press, 1991).
6 European Environment Agency, *Air Quality in Europe*, 6.
7 European Environment Agency, *Report no. No 6/2013 NEC Directive Status Report 2012: EEA Technical Report* (Copenhagen, 2013).
8 Albert Weale *et al.*, *Environmental Governance in Europe: An Ever Closer Ecological Union?* (Oxford: Oxford University Press, 2000).
9 European Commission, *Water Framework Directive* (Brussels, 2010).
10 Corey Johnson, "Toward Post-Sovereign Environmental Governance," *Water Alternatives* 5, no. 1 (2012): 83–97.
11 Daniel Hering *et al.*, "The European Water Framework Directive at the Age of 10: A Critical Review of the Achievements with Recommendations for the Future," *Science of the Total Environment* 408, no. 19 (2010): 4007–19.
12 European Commission, *A Blueprint to Safeguard Europe's Water Resources* (Brussels, 2012).
13 European Commission, *A Blueprint to Safeguard Europe's Water Resources.*
14 European Commission, *Report from the Commission to the European Parliament and the Council on the Implementation of the Water Framework Directive (2000/60/EC): River Basin Management Plans, COM (2012),* 670 Final (2012).
15 Duncan Liefferink, Mark Wiering and Yukina Uitenboogaart, "The EU Water Framework Directive: A Multi-Dimensional Analysis of Implementation and Domestic Impact," *Land Use Policy* 28, no. 4 (2011): 712–22.
16 European Environment Agency, *European Waters: Current States and Future Challenges* (Copenhagen, 2012).
17 Eurostat, *Environmental Statistics and Accounts in Europe* (Luxembourg: European Union, 2010), 99.
18 Henrik Selin, *Global Governance of Hazardous Chemicals: Challenges of Multilevel Management* (Cambridge, Mass.: MIT Press, 2010).
19 Seven separately regulated waste streams are: 1) waste oils; 2) waste from the titanium dioxide industry; 3) agricultural use of sewage sludge; 4) batteries and accumulators; 5) packaging and packaging waste; 6)

polychlorinated biphenyls and polychlorinated terphenyls (PCB/PCT); and 7) end-of-life vehicles.

20 Henrik Selin and Stacy D. VanDeveer, "Politics of Trade and Environment in the European Union," in *Handbook on Trade and Environment*, ed. Kevin P. Gallagher (Aldershot: Edward Elgar, 2008), 194–203.

21 Weale *et al.*, *Environmental Governance in Europe*.

22 The 10 WEEE product categories are: 1) large household appliances; 2) small household appliances; 3) IT and telecommunications equipment; 4) consumer equipment and photovoltaic panels; 5) lighting equipment; 6) electrical and electronic tools; 7) toys, leisure and sports equipment; 8) medical devices; 9) monitoring and control instruments; 10) automatic dispensers.

23 The six RoHS substances are: 1) lead; 2) mercury; 3) cadmium; 4) hexavalent chromium; 5) polybrominated biphenyls; and 6) polybrominated diphenyl ethers.

24 C. Jackson and E. Watkins, "EU Waste Law: The Challenge of Better Compliance," *Directions in European Environmental Policy* No. 5 (Brussels: Institute for European Environmental Policy, 2012).

25 European Commission, *Report from the Commission to the European Parliament, the Council, the European Economic and Social Committee and the Committee of Regions on the Thematic Strategy on the Prevention and Recycling of Waste, COM (2011), 13 Final* (2011).

26 Henrik Selin and Stacy D. VanDeveer, "Raising Global Standards: Hazardous Substances and E-Waste Management in the European Union," *Environment* 48, no. 10 (2006): 6–18.

27 Selin, *Global Governance of Hazardous Chemicals*.

28 Henrik Selin, "Coalition Politics and Chemicals Management in a Regulatory Ambitious Europe," *Global Environmental Politics* 7, no. 3 (2007): 63–93.

29 Noelle Eckley and Henrik Selin, "All Talk, Little Action: Precaution and its Effects on European Chemicals Regulation," *Journal of European Public Policy* 11, no. 1 (2004): 78–105.

30 European Chemicals Agency, *General Report 2009: The Year of Preparations* (Helsinki, 2010).

31 European Commission, *Report from the Commission to the European Parliament, the Council, the European Economic and Social Committee and the Committee of the Regions in accordance with Article 117(4) of REACH and Article 46(2) of CLP, and a review of certain elements of REACH in line with Articles 75(2), 138(2), 138(3) and 138(6) of REACH, COM (2013), 049 Final* (2013).

32 Mark A. Pollack and Gregory C. Shaffer, *When Cooperation Fails: The International Law and Politics of Genetically Modified Foods* (Oxford: Oxford University Press, 2009); Luc Bodiguel and Michael Cardwell, eds, *The Regulation of Genetically Modified Organisms: Comparative Approaches* (Oxford: Oxford University Press, 2010).

33 Sarah Lieberman and Tim Gray, "The So-Called 'Moratorium' on the Licensing of new Genetically Modified (GM) Products by the European Union 1998–2004: A Study in Ambiguity," *Environmental Politics* 15, no. 4 (2006): 592–609.

34 European Commission, *Evaluation of the EU Legislative Framework in the Field of GM Food and Feed* (Brussels, 2010); European Commission, *Evaluation of the EU Legislative Framework in the Field of Cultivation of*

GMOs Under Directive 2001/18/EC and Regulations (EC) No 1829/2003, and the Placing on the Market of GMOs as or in Products Under Directive 2001/18/EC (Brussels, 2011).

35 See ec.europa.eu/food/dyna/gm_register/index_en.cfm.
36 European Commission, *Evaluation of the EU Legislative Framework in the Field of GM Food and Feed* (2010).
37 Charlie Dunmore, "EU Court Annuls Approval of BASF's Amflora GMO Potato," *Thomson Reuters*, 13 December 2013; Matt McGrath, "GM Even Safer than Conventional Food, Says Environment Secretary," *BBC News*, 20 June 2013.
38 Dunmore, "EU Court Annuls Approval of BASF's Amflora GMO Potato."
39 David Vogel, *The Politics of Precaution: Regulating Health, Safety, and Environmental Risks in Europe and the United States* (Princeton, N.J.: Princeton University Press, 2012).
40 BBC, *Q&A: Reform of EU Farm Policy*, 1 July 2013, www.bbc.co.uk/news/world-europe-11216061.
41 European Commission, *The Common Agricultural Policy (CAP) and Agriculture in Europe—Frequently Asked Questions* (Brussels, June 2013).
42 European Commission, *The Common Agricultural Policy (CAP) and Agriculture in Europe—Frequently Asked Questions* (August 2013), ec.europa.eu/agriculture/faq/index_en.htm.
43 European Commission, *The Common Agricultural Policy (CAP) and Agriculture in Europe.*
44 Lee Ann Patterson, "Agricultural Policy Reform in the European Community: A Three-level Game Analysis," *International Organization* 51, no. 1 (1997): 135–65.
45 *The Local*, "Sweden: 'Abolish EU Farm Subsidies'," 29 May 2007.
46 Kate O'Neill, "Mad Cows and Ailing Hens: The Transatlantic Relationship and Livestock Diseases," in *Transatlantic Environment and Energy Politics: Comparative and International Perspectives*, ed. Miranda A. Schreurs, Henrik Selin and Stacy D. VanDeveer (Aldershot: Ashgate, 2009).
47 Matthias Stolze and Nicolas Lampkin, "Policy for Organic Farming: Rationale and Concepts," *Food Policy* 34, no. 3 (2009): 237–44.
48 Kendra Klein and David E. Winickoff, "Organic Regulation Across the Atlantic: Emergence, Divergence, Convergence," *Environmental Politics* 20, no. 2 (2011): 153–72.
49 European Commission, *The Common Agricultural Policy (CAP) and Agriculture in Europe.*
50 European Commission, *Facts and Figures of the Common Fisheries Policy: Basic Statistical Data* (Brussels, 2012).
51 European Environment Agency, *The European Environment State and Outlook 2010: Marine and Coastal Environment* (Copenhagen, 2010).
52 European Commission, *Facts and Figures of the Common Fisheries Policy* (2012).
53 European Environment Agency, *The European Environment State and Outlook 2010* (2010).
54 Tim Daw and Tim Gray, "Fisheries Science and Sustainability in International Policy: A Study of the Failure in the European Union's Common Fisheries Policy," *Marine Policy* 29, (2005): 189–97.

55 Elizabeth DeSombre and Samuel J. Barkin, *Saving Global Fisheries: Reducing Capacity to Promote Sustainability* (Cambridge, Mass.: MIT Press, 2013), 67.

56 Daw and Gray, "Fisheries Science and Sustainability in International Policy," 189–97.

57 DeSombre and Barkin, *Saving Global Fisheries*, 29, 115.

58 Commission, *Communication from the Commission to the European Parliament, the Council, the Economic and Social Committee and the Committee of the Regions. Our Life Insurance, Our Natural Capital: An EU Biodiversity Strategy to 2020, COM (2011), 244 Final* (2011).

59 European Environment Agency, *Protected Areas in Europe—An Overview* (Copenhagen, 2012).

60 G. Kristin Rosendal, "Global Biodiversity Governance: Genetic Resources, Species and Ecosystems," in *The Global Environment: Institutions, Law and Policy*, ed. Regina S. Axelrod and Stacy D. VanDeveer (Washington, DC: Sage/CQ Press, 2015).

61 Commission Communication, COM (2011) 244 Final.

62 European Commission, *EU Biodiversity Strategy to 2020* (Brussels, 2011).

63 Tanja Börzel and Aron Buzogány, "Environmental Organisations and the Europeanisation of Public Policy in Central and Eastern Europe: The Case of Biodiversity Governance," *Environmental Politics* 19, no. 5 (2010): 708–35.

64 European Environment Agency, *Protected Areas in Europe* (2012).

65 Secretariat to the Convention on Biological Diversity, *Global Biodiversity Outlook 3* (Montreal, 2010).

66 European Commission, *Flash Eurobarometer Series #290: Attitudes of Europeans Towards the Issue of Biodiversity, Wave 2*, 2010, ec.europa.eu/public_opinion/flash/fl_290_en.pdf.

67 See data.worldbank.org/indicator/EN.ATM.CO2E.PC.

68 Andrew Jordan *et al.*, eds, *Climate Change Policy in the European Union: Confronting the Dilemmas of Mitigation and Adaptation* (Cambridge: Cambridge University Press, 2010).

69 Elin Lerum Boasson and Jørgen Wettestad, *EU Climate Policy: Industry, Policy Interaction and External Environment* (Farnham: Ashgate, 2013).

70 European Commission, *The EU Emissions Trading Scheme (EU ETS)* (Brussels, 2013).

71 Corey Johnson and Tim Boersma, "Energy (In)security in Poland? The Case of Shale Gas," *Energy Policy* 53 (2013): 389–99.

72 European Environment Agency, *Trends and Projections in Europe 2013: Tracking Progress Towards Europe's Climate and Energy Targets Until 2020* (Copenhagen, 2013).

6 The EU abroad

- Gaining international legal status
- Global environmental politics
- Regional and transnational environmental cooperation
- Transatlantic relations and environmental policy
- Free trade, market access and foreign assistance

As EU officials and European politicians aspire to make the EU a globally recognized leader in environmental policy and sustainability, ambitions and influence reach well beyond external borders. Illustrating these international political aspirations, the Lisbon Treaty created the new post of High Representative of the Union for Foreign Affairs and Security Policy and established the EEAS to coordinate the common foreign and security policy as the EU's diplomatic arm. In much environmental and trade politics the European Commission acts on behalf of the EU. The Council of the European Union plays a central role in the EU's formulation of external environmental policy positions, and the European Parliament saw its intra-EU involvement in international environmental affairs expanded by the Lisbon Treaty. In addition, the EU maintains offices around world—including in national capitals such as Washington, DC, Beijing, Brasilia, New Delhi, and Pretoria—through which representatives promote the EU's political, economic, and environmental views and interests. EU environmental law also puts restrictions on types and contents of goods exported from outside countries into the single market.

This chapter analyzes the EU roles in global, regional, transnational and bilateral environmental politics, and discusses the EU's ability to promote its interests and achieve its policy goals in external relations. The next section discusses the evolution of the EU's international legal status and competences, allowing it to act independently on behalf of its member states in multilateral and bilateral settings on issues where the EU has exclusive and shared competence as outlined by the Lisbon Treaty. This is followed by discussion of EU activities in global environmental forums and treaty making. The subsequent section focuses on the EU's active role in regional environmental cooperation, including joining a long list of agreements, engaging countries seeking EU membership and others located near the Union's external borders. The chapter then looks at transatlantic environmental relations, followed by a discussion of market, trade-related and foreign assistance issues in the EU's bilateral interactions with countries around the world.

Gaining international legal status

The EU's ability to be active in international cooperation is dependent on fulfilling similar criteria as nation-states under international law.[1] First, the EU must possess legal personality. Already the EEC (through the Rome Treaty) and later the EC (in the SEA) were given legal competence by member states to engage external actors and forums on behalf of the Community. The Lisbon Treaty bestowed such legal personality on the EU. Second, the EU must be recognized as legitimately representing its member states by others. The EEC began the political process of gaining formal recognition from the international community. Since the 1970s, in the United Nations (UN) and other forums, the EEC/EC/EU is referred to as a Regional Economic Integration Organization. This label is not reserved exclusively for the EU, but no other intergovernmental organization has taken advantage of this opportunity. In addition, the EU has formal membership status in several major organizations, including UN bodies, the WTO, the African Union and the G20. One vehicle for this growing acceptance has been the EU's willingness to bring financial resources to cash-strapped international initiatives.

Third, the EU must possess internal competence to make legally binding commitments with third parties. Such EU authority varies greatly across the three levels of competences outlined in the Lisbon Treaty. In policy areas where supranational institutions are the strongest and the EU has exclusive competence, including adopting free trade agreements under the WTO, the European Commission is the sole negotiator with external partners on behalf of all member states. In what remain predominantly intergovernmental issue areas such as the formulation of security policy, where the EU (via the EEAS) merely has supporting competence, member state national governments retain the right to negotiate and conclude international agreements with third parties on their own behalf without EU interference. In between these two, in policy areas where the EU shares competences with member states (like environmental issues), the European Commission engages international affairs alongside member states' national delegations, resulting in "mixed agreements."[2] The EU's authority to conclude such agreements has expanded over time.

The fact that the Rome Treaty did not give the EEC authority over environmental issues initially limited the European Commission's ability to engage in external relations in this area. The Court of Justice played a critical role in changing this. In a 1971 milestone ruling in the case of the European Commission versus the Council of Ministers over the European Agreement on Road Transport, judges determined a critical link between internal and external powers. The ruling stated that in areas where the EEC had been given the authority to legislate internally, it had also implicitly been given powers to act externally. Through subsequent rulings and ensuing practice, this authority was expanded to apply to issue areas with no collective policy, but where EEC external participation was "necessary for the attainment of one of the objectives of the Community" as laid down in EEC laws and treaties.[3] The SEA moved beyond such case law and formally enshrined EC powers of external representation on environmental issues in the core treaties.

The EEC initially struggled to speak with a unified voice in international environmental politics, as representatives of EU bodies and member states often failed to articulate and support a common position. This slowed international recognition of the EEC by non-member countries that expressed uncertainty as to when they should negotiate with Brussels and when they should talk directly with member state national governments. More recently, the EU has improved its ability to present a relatively united front, but turf wars over authority and the right to speak between the European Commission and member states and differences in national interests can still hinder the EU's ability to act effectively in international forums on issues such as water pollution, the protection of the stratospheric ozone layer, climate change, and mercury abatement.[4] To be fair, however, large countries such as the United States sometimes experience similar challenges of intra-governmental communication and coordination in international affairs.

Global environmental politics

The EU frequently uses its political and economic "soft power"—as a normative or civilian power—to shape global policy debates and decisions based on norms relating to democracy, free markets, environmental protection and sustainable development.[5] EU actions are also driven by a desire to defend economic interests and enhance international regulatory competition.[6] Since the early 1990s, the EU has been at the forefront of global environmental politics, exhibiting three common types of leadership.[7] EU *structural leadership* comes from its ability and willingness to commit material resources in support of work by international organizations and scientific and technical advisory panels, shaping their operations and policy outcomes. The EU shows *entrepreneurial leadership* as representatives use their negotiating skills to influence how issues are framed and ultimately decided. The EU demonstrates *intellectual leadership* by diffusing ideas and knowledge to shape the way issues and policy alternatives are conceptualized and discussed in different venues. EU officials often combine two or more of these leadership forms in efforts to increase their impact: sometimes such efforts are more successful than others.[8]

Global forums

EU attempts at leadership are illustrated by repeated efforts to shape global policy goals based on internal initiatives and political ambitions. For example, the EU used a goal adopted by the European Council in 2001 to halt the regional decline of biodiversity by 2010 as a springboard to an agreement to reduce significantly the rate of biodiversity loss globally by 2010, at the Johannesburg Summit on Sustainable Development in 2002 and also included in the Millennium Development Goals. Rooted in the goal in the 2001 Sustainable Development Strategy that within a generation chemicals should be produced and used in ways that do not lead to a significant impact on health and the environment, the EU secured acceptance of a similar global goal (by 2020), also at the 2002 Johannesburg summit. Similarly, the EU's advocacy for UN recognition of the 2°C target for climate change was based on its 2007 adoption by the European Council. Yet, the 2010 biodiversity goal was missed, the 2020 chemicals goal will most likely not be met, and the 2°C target slips further out of reach with each passing year. Thus, while EU influence on global agreements is often clear, its impact on global environmental outcomes remains decidedly mixed, in part because global environmental institutions remain weak.

Both the extent and limit of the EU's leadership ambitions in global environmental politics and policymaking can be witnessed in major institutional reform processes. In continuing discussions about the possible creation of a World Environment Organization to replace UNEP, the EU and active member states such as Germany and France championed efforts to expand UNEP's mandate and operational scope. This leadership has shaped debate around these issues, but resulted in very limited organizational change in the face of strong resistance from other states.[9] Similarly, EU support was important in the creation of the UN Commission on Sustainable Development after the 1992 Rio conference, as well as its recent replacement by a new High-Level Political Forum. The EU also joined the 2009 International Renewable Energy Agency located in Abu Dhabi—a forum for political and technical cooperation to expand renewable energy generation. However, these institutional reforms and initiatives did not always go as far in establishing strong organizational structures as EU negotiators wanted.[10]

The EU is deeply engaged in political initiatives better to integrate environmental issues and sustainable development into the mandates and operations of leading economic organizations, including the World Bank and the many regional development banks. In the WTO, DG Trade and EU member states back the "new trade agenda" in which multilateral agreements should reduce political and economic barriers to trade and also cover broader social and environmental aspects of production and trade.[11] Thus trade agreements would set common rules on investment security, intellectual property rights, services, labor standards, and environmental protection, for example (consistent with notions of weak sustainability). Parallel EU efforts to push environmental, economic and social issues in multilateral economic forums have, however, been met with resistance from countries preferring the status quo.[12] As a result, EU negotiators were forced to accept compromises that fall well short of formal EU policy positions. Also, the European Commission and member states disagree over specific trade policy positions, not least on reducing agricultural subsidies within the CAP.[13]

The European Commission and member states extend political, financial, organizational and technical support to civil society organizations, from both inside and outside the EU, for participation in global forums (similar to the ways European non-state groups receive public assistance to partake in EU debates and stakeholder consultations).[14] This helps open state-centric processes and events and increase public participation at multilateral summits to participants from across Europe and the developing world. The European Commission and member states argue that backing civil society organizations is important to support democratization and sustainable development.[15] Such extensive and direct assistance to civil society groups is almost uniquely European. While many of the world's democratic countries express political support for greater inclusion of non-state actors in global environmental governance, it is much less common for non-European countries such as the United States and Japan to offer material aid to non-state actors to prepare and participate in global political processes.

Global treaty making

The European Commission began engaging global environmental law making in the 1980s as its internal authority to do so and its external acceptance by non-EU countries grew (see Table 6.1). The EU also became more involved in treaties that predate the 1980s, including those related to wetlands, endangered species, and pollution and dumping at sea. The EU record of environmental treaty membership is rivaled by few states outside Europe—in stark contrast to the US record, for example.[16] That environmental treaties fall within the EU category of mixed agreements has internal and external consequences for negotiation, signing, ratification, and implementation. Before the EU partakes in multilateral negotiations, internal discussions take place within and between the European Commission and the Council of the European Union. Formally, the European Commission proposes a negotiating mandate for discussion and possible amendment in sub-groups before approval by the Environmental Council. In this process, different DGs and member states often express varying opinions and interests that require accommodation.

EU representation in environmental treaty negotiations is shared by European Commission officials from DG Environment and other units, and a member state "troika" made up representatives from the country holding the Presidency of the European Council and the previous and next Presidency holders. Other member states participate as sovereign nations. The rotating European Council Presidency often relies heavily on lead states and European Commission staff who bring issue- and venue-specific expertise and continuity to EU representation and negotiating positions.[17] In general, the European Commission speaks on issues covered by EU competences and member states on the remaining ones.[18] However, determining who has the right to speak on a specific topic can involve open disagreement, as there are important differences across environmental issues. For example, the EU has a high degree of competence on international policy on the trade in hazardous wastes (as both trade and waste disposal issues are covered by EU laws), but less on climate change (where the EU has limited authority on energy supply and environmental/carbon taxation issues).[19]

International environmental agreements are signed by an EU official in parallel with a government representative of the member state holding the Presidency, and they must be ratified by both the EU and all member states individually. Historically, the only EU body involved in ratification was the Council of the European Union, with each individual member state more or less directly engaged in the initial

Table 6.1 Global environmental treaties and dates of EC/EU membership since 1985

Treaty	Date
• 1985 Vienna Convention for the Protection of the Ozone Layer	17 Oct. 1988
• 1987 Montreal Protocol on Substances that Deplete the Ozone Layer	16 Dec. 1988
• 1990 London Amendment (to the 1987 Montreal Protocol)	20 Dec. 1991
• 1992 Copenhagen Amendment (to the 1987 Montreal Protocol)	20 Nov. 1995
• 1997 Montreal Amendment (to the 1987 Montreal Protocol)	17 Nov. 2000
• 1999 Beijing Amendment (to the 1987 Montreal Protocol)	25 Mar. 2002
• 1989 Convention on the Transboundary Movement of Hazardous Wastes and their Disposal (Basel Convention)	7 Feb. 1994
• 1995 Ban Amendment	30 Sept. 1997
• 1999 Protocol on Liability and Compensation	Not a party
• 1992 Convention on Biological Diversity	21 Dec. 1993
• 2000 Cartagena Protocol on Biosafety	27 Aug. 2002
• 2010 Nagoya Protocol on Access to Genetic Resources and the Fair and Equitable Sharing of Benefits Arising from their Utilization	12 Oct. 2014
• 1992 UN Framework Convention on Climate Change	21 Dec. 1993
• 1997 Kyoto Protocol	31 May 2002
• 1994 UN Convention to Combat Desertification in Countries Experiencing Serious Drought and/or Desertification, Particularly in Africa	26 Mar. 1998
• 1998 Convention on the Prior Informed Consent Procedure for Certain Hazardous Chemicals and Pesticides in International Trade (Rotterdam Convention)	19 Dec. 2002
• 2001 Stockholm Convention on Persistent Organic Pollutants	16 Nov. 2004
• 2009 Statute of the International Renewable Energy Agency (IRENA)	13 July 2010
• 2013 Minamata Convention on Mercury	Not a party

formulation of the EU negotiating mandate and the evolving negotiations led by the European Commission. Since the Lisbon Treaty, the European Parliament must also consent before EU ratification is concluded. EU ratification means adjusting EU law to bring it into concurrence with international commitments, which may require amending existing laws or passing new ones through the ordinary legislative procedure. Like regular EU law, such legislative changes are to be implemented by all member states. However, treaty compliance faces domestic implementation problems and deficits similarly to those seen in other EU environmental law. Member states ratify international environmental treaties through processes stipulated in their national law.

EU officials often support the development of international legally binding agreements as a central means to address environmental problems. Like sovereign states engaged in such negotiations, EU negotiators typically work to fashion multilateral treaties that largely align with internal policies—in essence seeking to export components of the European regulatory state outside the Union as they push for rules and mandates consistent with EU legislation.[20] As the EU raised its internal standards across environmental issue areas, it increasingly pushed for relatively stringent mandates and provisions under global treaties. This often puts the EU at odds with other key global actors, such as the United States, Canada, Australia, Japan, China, India, and many other developing countries. This can be seen, for example, around persistent and sometimes acrimonious differences around climate change, biodiversity, GMOs, and the Law of the Sea. Even when the EU and other actors find broad agreement they often differ on a host of details requiring a series of compromises to conclude new multilateral agreements.

EU leadership in global environmental treaty making is visible in the strengthening controls on ozone-depleting substances under the Montreal Protocol and its many subsequent amendments. Trade and management measures on hazardous wastes have been expanded under the 1989 Basel Convention in large part due to EU backing. The EU similarly championed negotiations of the Rotterdam, Stockholm and Minamata Conventions on hazardous chemicals and heavy metals, and has been critical in expanding the number of substances regulated under the first two of these during their implementation. Under the UNFCCC and the Kyoto Protocol, the EU has advocated for mandatory controls on GHG emissions for all major industrialized countries. The EU supports the biodiversity convention, playing central roles designing mechanisms to address trade in living modified organisms and sharing of benefits from the use of genetic resources under the two related protocols. The EU also provides resources under the desertification convention, despite this being a limited problem in most of Europe.

In the formulation and implementation of treaty commitments, EU officials often advocate the application of legal principles central in EU environmental law. For example, EU representatives frequently refer to the precautionary principle in relation to climate change cooperation, the mitigation of hazardous substances, and the handling of GMOs.[21] The principle of common but differentiated responsibility is applied to the designation of global abatement obligations between industrialized and developing countries on ozone, GHGs, chemicals, and mercury, similar to the ways in which the efforts sharing principle is used in EU climate change policy. These efforts can be controversial. The EU and the United States in particular often disagree about how and where to refer to the precautionary principle in major treaties. The EU often faces opposition from industrialized and developing countries in negotiating country-specific mandates and responsibilities, where developing countries supportive of differentiated obligations also argue that wealthy countries (including those in Europe) do not take on strong enough obligations consistent with the polluter pays principle.[22]

A final form of EU influence worthy of attention relates to financing global treaty activities and bodies. The EU supports the Global Environment Facility, the primary multilateral financial mechanism for the conventions on biodiversity, climate change, desertification, persistent organic pollutants, and mercury, as well as the Montreal Protocol Multilateral Fund. The United States and Japan are the two largest individual donors to these funding mechanisms, followed by Germany, the UK and France, but total EU member state contributions exceed those collectively given by the United States and Japan.[23] EU programs offer co-financing for environmental and sustainable development projects, and member states are among those most likely to contribute additional voluntary funds to treaty bodies. Such funding is central to support developing country participation and carry out political, scientific and technical activities under major treaties. Certainly, developing countries and advocacy groups are correct when they argue that industrialized countries have failed to raise the funds necessary for better implementation of many environmental treaties, but the EU and its member states have donated a significant share of total funds raised to date.

Regional and transnational environmental cooperation

As environmental and sustainable development issues gained salience in EU politics, they featured more prominently in the EU's external relations on the European continent and beyond. Regional environmental and sustainability governance is a growing phenomenon around the world, and initiatives outside Europe are often shaped by European models and receive European assistance.[24] These issues are intertwined with strategic EU efforts to spread its influence beyond its expanding borders. The EU engages regional and transnational cooperation through multiple, multilevel means, including supporting environmental agreements and programs, gradually expanding its membership, and engaging non-members through multilateral and bilateral initiatives that either exclusively or partially center on environmental and sustainable development issues. These efforts can be controversial, especially outside the Union, as EU assistance often comes with highly specific conditions for recipient countries. At the same time, many outside countries actively seek EU support and access to the single market as part of their foreign policy strategies.

Regional agreements

Since the first EAP, the European Commission has stressed the importance of engaging regional forums and formulating common environmental policy positions. The European Commission also began using its expanded external mandate as European non-EEC countries recognized its competence to negotiate on environmental issues. In 1975 the EEC joined the Paris Convention for the Prevention of Marine Pollution from Land-based Sources as a full party to an environmental agreement for the first time. Since then, the EU has participated in the development and strengthening of a multitude of regional environmental treaties that include both member and non-member states (see Table 6.2). However the European Commission's vision of a greatly expanded role for itself in external affairs is not always supported by member states. In one example of internal tensions, member states refused to approve a new EEC directive on the dumping of waste at sea proposed by the European Commission partly to enable it to join the Oslo and London Conventions because they were reluctant to give the European Commission greater authority in these forums.[25]

Occasional internal disagreements notwithstanding, the EU is increasingly active in environmental cooperation in European sub-regions, in the EU periphery, and in areas around the world, including North Africa, Asia, the Arctic, and Antarctica. Starting in the 1970s, the EEC supported regional seas agreements around the Baltic and Mediterranean seas, and the North-East Atlantic, and river basin management schemes for the Danube and Rhine rivers. The EEC often

Table 6.2 Major regional environmental treaties since 1974 and ECC/EC/EU membership[26]

Treaty	Date
• 1974 Convention for the Prevention of Marine Pollution from Land-based Sources (Paris Convention)	3 Mar. 1975
• 1976 Convention for the Protection of the Mediterranean Sea Against Pollution (Barcelona Convention)	16 Mar. 1978
• 1976 Protocol on Dumping from Ships and Aircraft	16 Mar. 1978
• 1976 Protocol on Emergency Cooperation	19 May 1981
• 1980 Protocol on Land-based Sources	7 Oct. 1983
• Protocol on Specially Protected Areas	30 June 1984
• Protocol on Offshore Exploration and Exploitation	27 Feb. 2013
• 1995 Protocol on Specially Protected Areas (replacing the 1982 Protocol)	12 Nov. 1999
• 1996 Protocol on Land-Based Sources and Activities (replacing 1980 Protocol)	11 May 2008
• 1996 Protocol on Hazardous Wastes	Not a party
• 2002 Protocol on Preventing Pollution from Ships and Emergency (replacing the 1976 Protocol)	29 Apr. 2004
• 2008 Protocol on Integrated Coastal Zone Management in the Mediterranean	29 Sept. 2010
• 1976 Convention for the Protection of the Rhine Against Chemical Pollution	25 July 1977
• 1979 Convention on the Conservation of European Wildlife and Natural Habitats	7 May 1982
• 1979 Convention on the Conservation of Migratory Species of Wild Animals	1 Nov. 1983
• 1979 Convention on Long-range Transboundary Air Pollution (CLRTAP)	15 July 1982
• 1984 Protocol on Long-term Financing of the Cooperative Programme (EMEP)	29 Oct. 1984
• 1985 Protocol on Sulphur Emissions	Not a party
• 1988 Protocol on Nitrogen Oxides	17 Dec. 1993
• 1991 Protocol on Volatile Organic Compounds	Not a party
• 1994 Protocol on Further Reductions of Sulphur Emissions	24 Apr. 1998
• 1998 Protocol on Heavy Metals	3 May 2001
• 1998 Protocol on Persistent Organic Pollutants	20 Apr. 2004
• 1999 Protocol on Acidification, Eutrophication, and Ground-level Ozone	23 June 2003
• 1980 Convention on the Conservation of Antarctic Marine Living Resources	21 Apr. 1982

Treaty	Date
• 1983 Agreement for Cooperation in Dealing with Pollution of the North Sea by Oil and other Harmful Substances (Bonn Agreement)	24 Sept. 1984
• 1990 Cooperation Agreement for the Protection of the Coasts and Waters of the North-East Atlantic Against Pollution	28 Oct. 1993
• 2008 Additional Protocol	30 Oct. 2010
• 1991 Convention on Environmental Impact Assessment in a Trans-boundary Context (Espoo Convention)	24 June 1997
• 1991 Convention on the Protection of the Alps	26 Feb. 1996
• 1994 Protocol on Spatial Planning and Sustainable Development	Not a party
• 1994 Protocol on Conservation of Nature and the Countryside	Not a party
• 1994 Protocol on Mountain Farming	Not a party
• 1996 Protocol on Mountain Forests	Not a party
• 1998 Protocol on Tourism	6 July 2006
• 1998 Protocol on Energy	27 June 2006
• 1998 Protocol on Soil Conservation	6 July 2006
• 2000 Protocol on Transport	Not a party
• 1992 Convention on the Protection of the Marine Environment of the Baltic Sea Area (Helsinki Convention; replacing a 1974 Helsinki Convention)	20 Sept. 1994
• 1992 Convention for the Protection of the Marine Environment of the North-East Atlantic (OSPAR Convention; replacing the 1974 Paris Convention)	5 Nov. 1997
• 1992 Convention on the Transboundary Effects of Industrial Accidents	24 Apr. 1998
• 1992 Convention on the Protection and use of Transboundary Water-courses and International Lakes	14 Sept. 1995
• 1999 Protocol on Water and Health	Not a party
• 2003 Protocol on Civil Liability	Not a party
• 1994 Convention on Cooperation for the Protection and Sustainable Use of the River Danube	18 Dec. 1997
• 1995 Agreement on the Conservation of African-Eurasian Migratory Waterbirds	1 Oct. 2005
• 998 Convention on Access to Environmental Information, Public Par-ticipation in Decision-making and Access to Justice in Environmental Matters (Aarhus Convention)	17 Feb. 2005
• 1999 Convention on the Protection of the Rhine (replacing a 1963 Agreement and the 1976 Rhine Convention)	17 Nov. 2000
• 2003 Protocol on Pollutant Release and Transfer Registers	21 Feb. 2006
• 2010 Agreement on the Protection and Sustainable Development of the Prespa Park Area	Not a party

first engaged such efforts as observer, with the EU joining as a party later. The regional seas and river basin regimes became models for subsequent regional cooperation around the world.[27] Also starting in the 1970s, the EEC became involved in several regional agreements around nature conservation and air pollution abatement, including CLRTAP which brought Western and Eastern European states, as well as Canada, the United States, and the Soviet Union together. Beginning in the 1990s, many new and updated regional agreements made sustainable development a key objective, consistent with policy developments within the EU.

EU involvement and influence in regional environmental agreements grew over time. As in global forums, the EU often relies on its soft power to strategically combine structural, entrepreneurial, and intellectual forms of leadership in efforts to shape regional policy processes. This is clearly seen in air pollution work under CLRTAP, particularly as the development of pollution-specific protocols intersects with the evolution of EU air policy.[28] The European Commission and green leader states have repeatedly sought to raise regional and national emission reduction goals, while working to align domestic targets for member states across both forums. To these ends, they make frequent use of collaborative scientific and technical assessment processes to identify ecological and human health problems and frame policy options relating to the development and implementation of CLRTAP protocols and EU laws.[29] This includes committing substantial political, financial and human resources to the development of the critical loads and levels approaches that currently guide much policymaking in both CLRTAP and the EU.

EU political, scientific and technical influence in regional agreements is also seen in other environmental issue areas. For example, EU law and standards around limiting environmental and human exposure to hazardous chemicals and heavy metals intersect with the many multilateral pollution reduction measures still taking place around shared seas and rivers. Here too, specific environmental standards, sustainable development goals, and implementation efforts are intentionally brought into accord with those of the EU, as related initiatives are financially supported by the EU and its member states.[30] These external measures to reduce emissions and discharges of dangerous substances are critical to meeting short-term and long-term EU targets for improved water quality under the WFD. Similarly, the fulfillment of EU biodiversity policy and nature conservation goals, including those expanding the Natura 2000 network of protected areas, depends on the successful implementation of many provisions under water, wildlife, Alpine, and land-use agreements that stretch beyond the borders of the Union.

Enlargements and neighbors

Perhaps the most significant and successful growth in EU influence on environmental policymaking and implementation over the past two decades lies in membership enlargement. The 1995 addition of Austria, Finland and Sweden added three green leader states to the EU, all of which have frequently worked with EU bodies and other leading member states to expand and strengthen EU environmental policies since joining. Even if this addition of three high regulation states resulted in important changes to internal policy-making dynamics and outcomes, the eastern and southern enlargements—those in 2004, 2007 and 2013—merit the most attention regarding the EU's external environmental influence. Membership negotiations with official candidate countries (Iceland, Montenegro and Turkey) also continues at varying pace, coordinated through DG European Neighborhood and Enlargement Negotiations, but Jean-Claude Juncker announced in 2014 as President-Elect of the European Commission that no new countries would be admitted into the EU for the next five years.[31]

EU dominance over applicant states starts long before the adoption of an accession treaty allowing another country to join the club. Membership processes, based on clear conditionality, are highly intrusive into the national affairs of candidate countries. Their national governments, during drawn-out and sometimes contentious negotiations with the European Commission, agree to make significant legal, political and organizational changes, with the "golden carrot" of full membership as the key incentive.[32] In membership negotiations, the full body of EU *acquis* is divided into issue-specific chapters and addressed separately. Current negotiations are organized around 35 such chapters, including agriculture and rural development (Chapter 11), food safety, veterinary, and phytosanitary policy (Chapter 12), fisheries (Chapter 13), transport policy (Chapter 14), energy (Chapter 15), and environment (Chapter 27). A chapter is "closed" when the European Commission is satisfied that a candidate country has transposed all related EU laws into its national legal system. Until the process is complete for all chapters, a country cannot join the EU.

For formerly communist and centrally planned countries, joining the EU is a massive endeavor involving large changes in virtually every area of law and regulation, including those connected to environment and sustainability. While domestic environmental policy and management must be harmonized with EU law, this is only the beginning. States with little history of public participation in politics and little private property, for example, must transform the processes by which law and regulation are formulated, implemented, enforced and monitored.[33] State taxation schemes, environmental enforcement mechanisms, and judicial systems must be changed, while public, private and civil society actors in candidate states react to political agendas set almost exclusively by EU bodies and the need to meet harmonization requirements. These processes frequently result in mixed messages and diverse results. For example, emissions of many industrial pollutants often decline and nature protection increases even as resource consumption, urban sprawl, and waste production increase substantially.

Ten years after the accession of Estonia, Latvia, Lithuania, Czech Republic, Hungary, Poland, Slovakia and Slovenia, their public and civil society institutions are radically transformed, even as they struggle to implement EU environmental laws. More recent entrants, Bulgaria, Romania and Croatia, succeeded in harmonizing most national laws with the EU *acquis*, but are only beginning to grapple with implementation and enforcement. While each new EU member attempts to enact the same set of environmental policies, outcomes vary substantially across states and societies.[34] Evidence of corruption related to the application of environmental law in many older and more recent member states has also emerged, remaining difficult to address from Brussels.[35] Potential new members Albania, Macedonia, Montenegro, Serbia and Turkey all face challenges for decades to come. Because Iceland is a stable Western democracy that has already harmonized many domestic environmental laws and standards with those of the EU, its necessary state and societal transformations in preparation for full membership are less dramatic, more comparable to the 1995 entrants.

The influence of EU environmental policy also extends beyond the member states, to the neighboring EFTA countries, Iceland, Liechtenstein, and Norway, via their inclusion in the European Economic Area, and through a series of bilateral agreements with Switzerland—all coordinated through the EEAS. In practice, this means that many EU environmental policies and standards, especially those related to the transfer of goods and provision of services across the single market, currently apply to up to 32 countries. As mentioned in the previous chapter, many EU environmental policy instruments shape public and private sector decisions in one or more EFTA countries. The EU GHG trading scheme includes Iceland, Liechtenstein, and Norway (but not Switzerland), and Norway is developing local river management plans in accordance with the WFD. Also, EFTA states and Turkey are members of the European Environment Agency, whose assessments generate scientific and technical data which help build environmental awareness and inform many European decision-making processes.

The European Neighbourhood Policy (ENP), run through the EEAS and launched in 2004, offers privileged relationships in the EU "neighborhood"—countries in close geographical proximity which, at least in the medium term, are not being offered membership.[36] As of 2014, it includes 16 countries located to the EU's east (Armenia, Azerbaijan, Belarus, Georgia, Moldova, and Ukraine) and south (Algeria, Egypt, Israel, Jordan, Lebanon, Libya, Morocco, Palestine, Syria, and Tunisia). It builds on bilateral agreements with each country, focusing on broad "good governance" issues including democracy, political stability, and economic prosperity. Rather than the EU's soft power approach which seeks to fashion mutually acceptable compromises, the ENP exhibits traits of "soft imperialism," explicitly seeking to promulgate EU norms and persuade participating countries—with smaller economies and less regulatory capacity—to converge unilaterally with EU laws and standards.[37] Here, there is no "golden carrot" of membership promised, but merely a "silver carrot" of financial support and policy-specific benefits, including greater access for exporting particular goods to the single market.[38]

The ENP is based on positive conditionality and the "more for more principle," where the "better" a country performs (i.e. the more it conforms to EU standards), the more financial grants (from the European Commission), loans (from the European Investment Bank and the European Bank for Reconstruction and Development), and policy benefits are offered as rewards. Country-specific agendas cover governance challenges relating to greater public access to information, policy expansions, and improved implementation on a host of environmental, energy and transportation issues including climate change, resource and waste management, hazardous chemicals, and water management (including enhanced national ratification and implementation of global and regional agreements in these areas). These countries' access to the single market also requires product-specific harmonization with EU environmental, consumer, and food safety standards. However, studies of the effectiveness of the ENP show mixed policy convergence across countries shaped by political and economic factors playing out across regional, national, and local levels.[39]

Public sector capacity building and civil society support

As EU initiatives seek to push neighborhood countries to adjust to EU standards and make substantial public and private sector changes toward more sustainable development, the Union invests substantial resources in support of state capacity building and training through a series of programs largely known by their (often cumbersome) acronyms.[40] These include PHARE (on democratization and economic restructuring), LIFE (facilitating financial investments for the environment), SAPARD (focusing on rural and agricultural development), and IPSA (centering on environment- and transportation-related infrastructure projects)—to name only a few. Billions of euros have been channeled through such programs, often co-financed by member states and multilateral development banks. These paid for discrete items, such as technological improvements in public sector organizations, training modules, and consultation and assessment services, as well as longer-term initiatives to improve public sector accountability, efficiency, planning, and stakeholder engagement.

The EU has been a key player in the UN Economic Commission for Europe (UNECE)-organized Environment for Europe process since the early 1990s. This political initiative seeks to play two main roles combining regional and country-based measures: 1) providing a political pan-European framework for environmental cooperation through the organization of ministerial conferences; and 2) promoting improved national capacities and policies to deal with environmental issues among UNECE member states.[41] Connected to the Environment for Europe process and earlier efforts by the Organisation for Economic Co-operation and Development (OECD), UNECE develops country-specific Environmental Performance Reviews, which combine expertise from the country's public sector with domestic stakeholders and outside experts to review a state's environmental performance, generate policy-relevant data, and set policy priorities. Assessed countries often work for years to reform aspects of law, policies and processes identified as needing improvement. Early such work with Central and Eastern European countries helped prepare them for EU membership. However, policy progress again varies substantially across environmental issue areas and participating countries.[42]

EU environment-related capacity-building programs, and those focused on democratization and economic reforms, also facilitate civil society development in candidate and ENP states.[43] Such political and material support takes many forms, including direct financial contributions, training and technical assistance for non-state groups, running programs encouraging public officials to include a broad range of stakeholders in policymaking and implementation processes, and backing "twinning" programs that pair civil society actors in recipient countries with more established groups from within the EU. For example, the European Commission was a founding donor in 1990 to help create the Regional Environment Center (REC) in Hungary, with a mission to build civil society capacities and enhance cooperation between public, private and civil society actors in domestic environmental decision making and implementation. European Commission backing for the REC continues, almost 25 years later, to support its work across Central and Eastern Europe, from the Baltic states in the north to Bulgaria and Turkey in the south.

Building on the original REC model, the EU helped establish a REC Caucasus office to support non-state activities in Azerbaijan, Armenia and Georgia. The REC Caucasus program, which engages national and local governments, interest groups, media, schools, and business, was established under the Environment for Europe process, which also prioritizes building civil society capacities and enhancing public participation in environmental decision making. Such support relates directly to the creation and implementation of the Aarhus Convention (see Table 6.2). It outlines publics' rights concerning information access and participation in public sector decision-making processes on local, national and transboundary environmental matters. By codifying such rights, it creates a legal basis for increased and improved interaction between citizens and public authorities. The European Commission views civil society as playing a central role in monitoring state actions and disseminating information; similar to the view that civil society groups fulfill important functions in the implementation of EU policy in member states. In short, EU programs aim to transform politics, as well as law and regulation in candidate and ENP countries.

Transatlantic relations and environmental policy

The many political, economic and social relationships between Europe and North America are densely institutionalized, linking public, private and civil society actors from local to regional scales. This close transatlantic relationship is based on the development of shared values over generations, as each region came to embrace many similar norms and interests embedded in democratic and free-market societies. Illustrating these deep bonds, the EU (through the EEAS) has formulated independent Strategic Partnerships with both the United States and Canada.[44] The two partnerships cover a broad range of political and economic topics. Environment and sustainable development issues are not always at the top of this agenda, but they have attained growing importance in recent decades. These areas include public disagreements over rule making, preferred goals, and influence in bilateral and multilateral forums.[45] Such transatlantic divergence results partly from different regional trends in policymaking, with the EU having taken a leadership position on many environmental issues.[46]

North American and European cooperation and competition are visible in many international environmental arenas. The United States and Canada, together with the EU, have offered political and financial support in the negotiation and implementation of major environmental treaties and international environmental organizations since the 1970s. However, the EU, Canada and United States frequently diverge over major policy initiatives and the formulation of specific mandates. Such disagreements have become more common since the early 1990s. Canadian and EU environmental treaty ratification patterns are generally similar, with the important exception of their respective positions on the Kyoto Protocol following Canadian withdrawal in 2011. Meanwhile, the United States has not joined the Basel, Stockholm and Rotterdam conventions on wastes and chemicals, the biodiversity agreements, or the Kyoto Protocol. Yet the United States was the first country to become a party to the Minamata Convention. Also, attention to sub-national policymaking dynamics on each side of the Atlantic reveals that the EU and North America have more in common on climate change than is apparent in high-level relations.[47]

The United States was an early global leader through the creation of the Environmental Protection Agency in 1970 and the passing of groundbreaking federal legislation such as the Clean Air Act (1970), the Clean Water Act (1972), and the Toxic Substances Control Act (1976), and championing many international environmental treaties in the 1970s and 1980s.[48] Ambitious US policies at this time influenced EU decision making on chemicals management and vehicle emissions, for example. Similarly, Canada's reputation as an early environmental frontrunner was built on the creation of the Department of Environment in 1971, the introduction of federal legislation on air and water pollution and toxic substances in the 1970s (including around the Great Lakes in bilateral cooperation with the United States), and for backing multilateral processes and organizations including UNEP.[49] Starting in the 1980s, however, the EU gradually took over the international leadership role based on a combination of the growing size of the single market, gaining greater capacity on environmental issues, internal expansions of environmental policy, and the emergence of strong anti-regulatory movements and stalled environmental agendas in Washington, DC and Ottawa.[50]

Environmental issues are also present in transatlantic trade and market integration. The 2013 EU and Canada free trade agreement eliminates tariffs on a wide range of industrial and agricultural products and expands market access in services and investment. A European Commission mandated Trade Sustainability Impact Assessment, since 1999 conducted before any new trade negotiations begin, discusses several environmental issues, including: GHG emissions from natural resource extraction (including oil from tar sands) and transportation; chemicals use, land-use changes, and water usage associated with higher agricultural output; and implications for marine environments from more integrated fisheries and seafood industries.[51] The Transatlantic Trade and Investment Partnership agreement being negotiated by the EU and United States may have significant environmental implications, if concluded. It touches on many well-known policy differences on, for example, GMO controls (also connected to WTO disputes) and restrictions of specific chemicals and heavy metals in consumer goods (related to the implementation of the REACH regulation and the WEEE and RoHS directives).

The two concurrent transatlantic trends—diverging environmental policy developments and deepening trade and market integration—raise questions about the future trajectories in environmental standards in Europe and North America. However, rather than one side always adjusting to the other, evidence suggests that hybridization is common, where legal approaches diffuse in both directions and shape new policies on both sides of the Atlantic.[52] US and Canadian governments and EU bodies frequently engage each other, competing to shape policy outcomes on issues such as product standards, GMO regulation, chemicals management, and controls of GHG emissions. Related to international environmental policy competition is a sharp increase in North American private sector lobbying in Brussels, as the EU market and regulatory influence grows in Europe and globally.[53] At the same time, the adoption of expansive transatlantic free trade agreements prohibiting discrimination on the basis of product and production methods may make it more difficult for one side to unilaterally introduce new environmental mandates that impact traded goods and services.

Finally, transatlantic relations involve expansive multilevel connections between environmental leaders in public, private and civil society sector in Europe and North America, with some US states and Canadian provinces leading on issues on which their federal authorities refuse to act and serving as channels for policy hybridization. For example, the European Commission, EU member states, US states, and Canadian provinces collaborate through the International Carbon Action Partnership, supporting the development of GHG trading schemes worldwide toward the creation of a global carbon market. Countries such as Sweden and the UK, as well as German *länder*, signed partnerships with US states to exchange best practices and collaborate on research, development, and trade in low-carbon technologies.[54] North American and European cities collaborate in several forums, including the Cities for Climate Protection program, the Clinton Foundation's Climate Initiative, and the C40 Cities program. Such initiatives diffuse information about mitigation and adaptation efforts and build local governance capacity in areas such as building standards, transportation, and waste management.[55]

Free trade, market access and foreign assistance

EU external relations engage countries also beyond its neighbors and North America, sometimes through Strategic Partnerships. To date, the EU has set up five multilateral partnerships with groups of countries and international organizations (Africa and the African Union, the Mediterranean and Middle East, Latin America and the Caribbean, the UN, and the North Atlantic Treaty Organization—NATO), and eight bilateral ones with Brazil, China, India, Japan, South Korea, Mexico, Russia, and South Africa. These reflect EU leadership ambitions and the EU's need to engage emerging powers based on varying degrees of cooperation and shared visions and interests.[56] EU relations with Russia and China are complex and sometimes overtly conflictual, while it has been easier to build close relationships with South Korea and Japan, for example. In these partnerships issues such as energy and climate change have gained increased salience, and may be used as bridge-building issues for expanded cooperation, with the EU financially supporting the development of related action plans, information sharing and technical assistance projects.[57]

Consistent with the Europe 2020 Strategy for creating a more innovative, resilient, and competitive Europe, the EU uses preferential agreements to increase access for European firms to foreign markets in industrialized and developing countries.[58] By 2013, the EU had concluded preferential trade agreements with over 50 countries (under the authority of DG Trade).[59] Many are with EFTA and neighboring countries, but several were signed with countries in the Americas, Africa and Asia. The EU also created a separate Generalised Scheme of Preferences which extends trade and financial assistance benefits to former European colonies and the world's least developed countries, including allowing their domestic firms to pay lower duties on exports to the EU, intended to support sustainable development in these countries.[60] Ongoing free trade negotiations involve not only the United States, but also Japan, India and others, and the EU and China launched talks in 2013 on an investment agreement.

The growing number of trade and investment agreements beyond the transatlantic region is an increasingly central means through which the EU explicitly engages an increasing number of countries on environment and sustainable development issues. Also in these external relations, EU bodies and member states back the new trade agenda where environmental issues are paid explicit attention in pre-negotiation Trade Sustainability Impact Assessments as well as subsequent trade and investment agreements.[61] As with ENP, these EU initiatives often embrace more of a "soft imperialism" than "soft power" position, trying to use access to the single market's many firms and consumers to leverage (or impose) adoption by other countries of environmental norms and standards close to those within the Union. The push to raise foreign standards also serves to ease some concerns by European politicians and industry representatives that EU regulatory expansion may negatively impact the ability of European businesses successfully to meet intensified competition in global markets from firms in emerging economies.[62]

Of course, it is easier for EU officials to take firm positions in negotiations with a small developing country than in talks with a stronger competitor like Japan. Such EU tactics can be met with substantial opposition from developing country officials, resisting external imposition of standards they believe should be set nationally.[63] Yet, EU bilateral trade agreements contain specific provisions on following multilateral labor and environmental standards, joining and effectively implementing major treaties, and preserving and protecting natural resources. The EU and its partners commit to monitor and assess impacts and the implementation of trade agreements on sustainable development, including through mechanisms that allow participation of civil society groups. Beyond formal agreements, countries outside Europe sometimes voluntarily use EU environmental standards as models for strengthening their own laws and regulations. For example, EU mandates on hazardous substances and European pollution control techniques have diffused to countries such as China, Japan, and South Korea, confirming that EU environmental policy often sets global standards.[64]

In addition, EU internal policies can have political, economic, and ecological consequences far beyond its borders. Ambitious biofuels and renewable energy mandates, for example, create import needs for many member states struggling to meet their national targets. Such demand can positively support rural employment and create much-needed income for poor farmers in developing countries. However, EU mandates may also contribute to land degradation and land disputes abroad, and lead to increased food insecurity.[65] European GMO rules and public attitudes influence cultivation and export decisions by farmers in countries looking to sell their products within the single market as well as in more GMO-friendly countries such as the United States. European corporate investment in overseas factories also produces mixed outcomes. In some cases it leads to the implementation of high environmental standards sometimes surpassing those in the EU, while in other instances it transmits European environmental problems abroad by, for example, contributing to overfishing around the globe.[66] More generally, high European consumption levels drive much resource use and pollution in countries facilitating these habits.

Finally, foreign development policy is another major mechanism through which the EU engages developing countries towards the overall objective of poverty eradication in the context of sustainable development. Northern European countries have long been global leaders in providing official development assistance and other forms of humanitarian support aimed at improving living conditions and opportunities for the world's poorest people. Even as the EU increases its role in setting aid priorities and coordinating activities, most such financial assistance still comes from member state national capitals.[67] Adding up official development assistance from all member states, the EU is the world's leading donor. Estimated for 2011, the EU-27 donated €53.1 billion—in comparison the United States and Japan donated €22.1 billion and €7.6 billion, respectively.[68] Nevertheless, for many developing countries the EU removal of trade barriers on agricultural products, including cutting CAP subsidies, is politically and economically more important than increases in development assistance.

Notes

1 Tom Delreux, *The EU as International Environmental Negotiator* (Aldershot: Ashgate, 2011); Alberta M. Sbragia, "Institution-Building from Below and Above: The European Community in Global Environmental Politics," in *European Integration and Supranational Governance*, ed. Wayne Sandholtz and Alec Stone Sweet (Oxford: Oxford University Press, 1998).
2 John Temple Lang, "The Ozone Layer Convention: A New Solution to the Question of Community Participation in 'Mixed' International Agreements," *Common Market Law Review* 23 (1986): 157–76.
3 John Vogler, "The European Union as an Actor in International Environmental Politics," *Environmental Politics* 8, no. 3 (1999): 30.
4 Nigel Haigh, "The European Community and International Environmental Policy," in *The International Politics of the Environment*, ed. Andrew Hurrell and Benedict Kingsbury (Oxford: Clarendon Press, 1992), 228–49; Richard E. Benedick, *Ozone Diplomacy: New Directions in Safeguarding the Planet* (Cambridge, Mass.: Harvard University Press, 1991), 35; Tom

Delreux, "The EU as an Actor in Global Environmental Politics," in *Environmental Policy in the EU: Actors, Institutions and Processes*, ed. Andrew Jordan and Camilla Adelle, third edn (London: Earthscan, 2013), 287–305.

5 Mai'a K. Davis Cross and Jan Melissen, eds, *European Public Diplomacy: Soft Power at Work* (New York: Palgrave Macmillan, 2013); Charlotte Bretherton and John Vogler, *The European Union as a Global Actor*, second edn (New York: Routledge, 2006); Simon Lightfoot and Jon Burchell, "The European Union and the World Summit on Sustainable Development: Normative Power Europe in Action?" *Journal of Common Market Studies* 43, no. 1 (2005): 75–95; Ian Manners, "Normative Power Europe: A Contradiction in Terms?" *Journal of Common Market Studies* 40, no. 2 (2002): 235–58.

6 R. Daniel Kelemen, "Globalizing European Union Environmental Policy," *Journal of European Public Policy* 17, no. 3 (2010): 335–49; Robert Falkner, "The Political Economy of 'Normative Power' Europe: EU Environmental Leadership in International Biotechnology Regulation," *Journal of European Public Policy* 14, no. 4 (2007): 507–26.

7 Oran R. Young, "Political Leadership and Regime Formation: On the Development of Institutions in International Society," *International Organization* 45, no. 3 (1991): 281–308.

8 Yves Tiberghien, ed., *Leadership in Global Institution Building: Minerva's Rule* (New York: Palgrave Macmillan, 2013).

9 Maria Ivanova, "Institutional Design and UNEP Reform: Historical Insights on Form, Function and Financing," *International Affairs* 88, no. 3 (2012): 565–84.

10 John Vogler and Hannes R. Stephan, "The European Union in Global Environmental Governance: Leadership in the Making?" *International Environmental Agreements* 7 (2007): 389–413.

11 Brigid Gavin, *The European Union and Globalisation: Towards Global Democratic Governance* (Cheltenham: Edward Elgar, 2001).

12 Björn-Ola Linnér and Henrik Selin, "The United Nations Conference on Sustainable Development: Forty Years in the Making," *Environment & Planning C: Government & Policy* 31, no. 6 (2013): 971–87.

13 Eugénia da Conceição-Heldt, "Variation in EU Member States' Preference and the Commission's Discretion in the Doha Round," *Journal of European Public Policy* 18, no. 3 (2011): 403–19.

14 Kim D. Reimann, "A View from the Top: International Politics, Norms and the Worldwide Growth of NGOs," *International Studies Quarterly* 50, no. 1 (2006): 45–67.

15 European Commission, *Communication from the European Commission to the European Parliament, the Council, the European Economic and Social Committee and the Committee of Regions: The Roots of Democracy and Sustainable Development: Europe's Engagement with Civil Society in External Relations, COM (2012)*, 492 (2012).

16 Miranda A. Schreurs, Henrik Selin and Stacy D. VanDeveer, "Expanding Transatlantic Relations: Implications for Environment and Energy Politics," in *Transatlantic Environment and Energy Politics: Comparative and International Perspectives*, ed. M.A. Schreurs, H. Selin and S.D. VanDeveer (Aldershot: Ashgate, 2009).

17 Tom Delreux and Karoline Van den Brande, "Taking the Lead: Informal Division of Labour in the EU External Environmental Policy-Making," *Journal of European Public Policy* 20, no. 1 (2013): 113–31.

18 Tom Delreux, "The EU as a Negotiator in Multiple Chemicals Negotiations: Multiple Principals, Different Agents," *Journal of European Public Policy* 15, no. 7 (2008): 1069–86.

19 John Vogler, "European Union Environmental Policy," in *Comparative Environmental Regionalism*, ed. Lorraine Elliot and Shaun Breslin (New York: Routledge, 2011), 19–36.

20 David Bach and Abraham L. Newman, "The European Regulatory State and Global Public Policy: Micro-Institutions, Macro-Influence," *Journal of European Public Policy* 14, no. 6 (2007): 827–46.

21 Henrik Selin and Stacy D. VanDeveer, "Global Climate Change: Beyond Kyoto," in *Environmental Policy: New Directions for the Twenty-First Century*, ed. N.J. Vig and M.E. Kraft, eighth edn (Washington, DC: CQ Press, 2013), 278–98; Henrik Selin, *Global Governance of Hazardous Chemicals: Challenges of Multilevel Management* (Cambridge, Mass.: MIT Press, 2010); Mark A. Pollack and Gregory C. Shaffer, *When Cooperation Fails: The International Law and Politics of Genetically Modified Foods* (Oxford: Oxford University Press, 2009).

22 Adil Najam, "A View from the South: Developing Countries in Global Environmental Politics," in *The Global Environment: Institutions, Law and Policy*, ed. Regina S. Axelrod and Stacy D. VanDeveer, fourth edn (Washington, DC: CQ Press, 2015), 213–31.

23 United Nations Environment Programme, *Status of Contributions and Disbursements*, 31 October 2013 (UNEP/OzL.Pro/ExComm71/3); GEF Secretariat, *Summary of Negotiations: Fifth Replenishment of the GEF Trust Fund*, 17 May 2010 (GEF/A.4/7).

24 Jörg Balsiger and Stacy D. VanDeveer, "Regional Governance for Environmental Problems," in *The International Studies Encyclopedia 9*, ed. Robert A. Denemark (Oxford: Blackwell Publishing, 2010), 6179–200; Lorraine Elliott and Shaun Breslin, eds, *Comparative Regional Environmental Governance* (London: Routledge, 2011).

25 Haigh, "The European Community and International Environmental Policy," 228–49.

26 The list of regional environmental treaties does not include bilateral environmental agreements or bilateral and multilateral fisheries and agriculture agreements.

27 Stacy D. VanDeveer, "Protecting Europe's Seas: Lessons from the Last 25 Years," *Environment* 42, no. 6 (2000): 10–26.

28 Henrik Selin and Stacy D. VanDeveer, "Institutional Linkages and European Air Pollution Politics," in *Governing the Air: The Dynamics of Science, Policy and Citizen Interaction*, ed. R. Lidskog and G. Sundqvist (Cambridge, Mass.: MIT Press, 2011), 61–92.

29 Alex Farrel, Stacy D. VanDeveer and Jill Jäger, "Environmental Assessments: Four Under-appreciated Elements of Design," *Global Environmental Change* 11, no. 4 (2001): 311–33.

30 Stacy D. VanDeveer, "Agenda Setting at Sea and in the Air," in *Improving Global Environmental Governance: Best Practices for Architecture and*

Agency, ed. Norichika Kanie, Steinar Andresen and Peter M. Haas (Abingdon: Routledge, 2014), 31–55.

31 Jean-Claude Juncker, *A New Start for Europe: My Agenda for Jobs, Growth, Fairness and Democratic Change*. Political Guidelines for the Next Commission. 15 July 2014. http://ec.europa.eu/about/juncker-commission/docs/pg_en.pdf.

32 Vogler, "European Union Environmental Policy," 19–36.

33 JoAnn Carmin and Stacy D. VanDeveer, eds, *EU Enlargement and the Environment: Institutional Change and Environmental Policy in Central and Eastern Europe* (Abingdon: Routledge, 2005).

34 Liliana B. Andonova and Stacy D. VanDeveer, "EU Expansion and the Internationalization of Environmental Politics," in *Comparative Environmental Politics*, ed. Paul F. Steinberg and Stacy D. VanDeveer (Cambridge, Mass.: MIT Press, 2012); Tanja A. Börzel, ed., *Coping With Accession to the European Union: New Modes of Environmental Governance* (Basingstoke: Palgrave Macmillan, 2009); John A. Scherpereel, "EU cohesion Policy and the Europeanization of Central and Eastern Regions," *Regional and Federal Studies* 20, no. 1 (2010): 45–62; Florian Bieber, ed., *EU Conditionality in the Western Balkans* (New York: Routledge, 2013).

35 Davide Torsello, *New Environmentalism? Civil Society and Corruption in the Enlarged EU* (Farnham: Ashgate, 2012).

36 Björn Hettne and Fredrik Söderbaum, "Civilian Power of Soft Imperialism? The EU as a Global Actor and the Role of Interregionalism," *European Foreign Affairs Review* 10, no. 4 (2005): 535–52; Karen E. Smith, "The Outsiders: The European Neighbourhood Policy," *International Affairs* 81, no. 4 (2005): 757–73.

37 Julia Langbein and Tanja A. Börzel, "Introduction: Explaining Policy Change in the European Union's Eastern Neighborhood," *Europe-Asia Studies* 65, no. 4 (2013): 571–80.

38 Vogler, "European Union Environmental Policy," 19–36.

39 Langbein and Börzel, "Introduction"; Aron Buzogány, "Selective Adoption of EU Environmental Norms in Ukraine: Convergence a la Carte," *Europe-Asia Studies* 65, no. 4 (2013): 609–30.

40 Carmin and VanDeveer, *EU Enlargement and the Environment*; Ron Linden, ed., *Norms and Nannies* (Lanham, Md.: Rowman & Littlefield, 2002); Liliana B. Andonova, *Transnational Politics of the Environment* (Cambridge, Mass.: MIT Press, 2004).

41 Ralf Nordbeck, "Pan-European Environmental Cooperation: Achievements and Limitations of the 'Environment for Europe' Process," in *Comparative Environmental Regionalism*, ed. Lorraine Elliot and Shaun Breslin (New York: Routledge, 2011), 37–55.

42 Liliana B. Andonova and Ioana A. Tuta, "Transnational Networks and Paths to EU Compliance: Evidence from New Member States," *Journal of Common Market Studies* 52, no. 4 (2014): 775–93.

43 Tanja A. Börzel and Aron Buzogány. "Governing EU Accession in Tranition Conutries: The Role of Non-State Actors," *Acta Politica* 45, no.1 (2010): 158–82; JoAnn Carmin, "NGO Capacity and Environmental Governance in Central and Eastern Europe," *Acta Politica* 45, no. 1 (2010): 182–202; Adam Fagan and JoAnn Carmin, eds, *Green Activism in Post-Socialist Europe and the Former Soviet Union* (New York: Routledge, 2011).

44 Carmen-Cristina Cîrlig, *EU Strategic Partnerships with Third Countries* (Luxembourg: European Parliamentary Research Service, 2012).

45 Schreurs *et al.*, "Expanding Transatlantic Relations."

46 R. Daniel Kelemen and David Vogel, "Trading Places: The Role of the United States and the European Union in International Environmental Politics," *Comparative Political Studies* 43, no. 4 (2010): 427–56; Norman J. Vig and Michael G. Faure, eds, *Green Giants? Environmental Policies of the United States and the European Union* (Cambridge, Mass.: MIT Press, 2004).

47 Henrik Selin and Stacy D. VanDeveer, "Federalism, Multilevel Governance and Climate Politics across the Atlantic," in *Comparative Environmental Politics*, ed. Paul F. Steinberg and Stacy D. VanDeveer (Cambridge, Mass.: MIT Press, 2012).

48 Sheldon Kamieniecki and Michael E. Kraft, eds, *Oxford Handbook on U.S. Environmental Politics* (Oxford: Oxford University Press, 2012).

49 Laurel Sefton MacDowell, *An Environmental History of Canada* (Vancouver: UBC Press, 2012).

50 Jon Birger Skjærseth, Guri Bang and Miranda A. Schreurs, "Explaining Growing Climate Policy Differences Between the European Union and the United States," *Global Environmental Politics* 13, no. 3 (2013): 61–80; David Vogel, *The Politics of Precaution: Regulating Health, Safety, and Environmental Risks in Europe and the United States* (Princeton, N.J.: Princeton University Press, 2012); Anu Bradford, "The Brussels Effect," *Northwestern University Law Review* 107, no. 1 (2012): 1–68.

51 See trade.ec.europa.eu/doclib/docs/2011/september/tradoc_148201.pdf.

52 Jonathan B. Wiener, "Convergence, Divergence, and Complexity in US and European Risk Regulation," in *Green Giants? Environmental Policies of the United States and the European Union*, ed. Norman J. Vig and Michael G. Faure (Cambridge, Mass.: MIT Press, 2004), 73–109.

53 Eric Lipton and Danny Hakim, "Lobbying Bonanza as Firm Try to Influence European Union," *The New York Times*, 13 October 2013.

54 Holley Andrea Ralston, *Subnational Partnerships for Sustainable Development: Transatlantic Cooperation Between the United States and Germany* (Cheltenham: Edward Elgar, 2013).

55 Henrik Selin and Stacy D. VanDeveer, "Multilevel Governance and Transatlantic Climate Change Politics," in *Greenhouse Governance: Addressing American Climate Change Policy*, ed. Barry G. Rabe (Washington, DC: Brookings Institution Press, 2010), 336–52.

56 Cîrlig, *EU Strategic Partnerships with Third Countries.*

57 David Scott, "Environmental Issues as a 'Strategic' Key in EU-China Relations," *Asia Europe Journal* 7, no. 2 (2009): 211–24; Emily Murrell, *The European Union's Role in the Formation of India's Climate Change Policy* (Bruges Regional Integration & Global Governance Papers, 2012); Stavros Afionis and Lindsay C. Stringer, *The Environment as a Strategic Priority in the European Union—Brazil Partnership: Is the EU Behaving as a Normative Power or Soft Imperialist?* (Leeds: Sustainability Research Institute, 2012).

58 Brigid Gavin and Alice Sindzingre, "EU Trade Relations with Emerging Asia: Identifying the Issue," *Asia Europe Journal* 7, no. 1 (2009): 9–22.

59 European Commission, *The EU's Bilateral Trade and Investment Agreements—Where are We? MEMO (13) 1080* (December 2013).

60 Morten Broberg, *The EU's Legal Ties with its Former Colonies: When Old Love Never Dies* (Copenhagen: DIIS Working Paper, 2011), 01.

61 Sikina Jinnah and Elisa Morgera, "Environmental Provisions in American and EU Free Trade Agreements: A Preliminary Comparison and Research Agenda," *Review of European Community and International Environmental Law* 22, no. 3 (2013): 324–39; Henrik Horn, Petros C. Mavroidis and André Sapir, "Beyond the WTO? An Anatomy of EU and US Preferential Trade Agreements," *The World Economy* 33, no. 11 (2010): 1565–88.

62 European Commission, *Report from the Commission to the European Parliament, the Council, the European Economic and Social Committee and the Committee of the Regions in accordance with Article 117(4) of REACH and Article 46(2) of CLP, and a review of certain elements of REACH in line with Articles 75(2), 138(2), 138(3) and 138(6) of REACH, COM (2013), 049 Final* (2013).

63 Kevin P. Gallagher, "Understanding Developing Country Resistance to the Doha Round," *Review of International Political Economy* 15, no. 1 (2008): 62–85.

64 Henrik Selin, "Minervian Politics and International Chemicals Policy," in *Leadership in Global Institution Building: Minerva's Rule*, ed. Yves Tiberghien (New York: Palgrave Macmillan, 2013), 193–212.

65 Mairon G. Bastos Lima and Joyeeta Gupta, "The Policy Context of Biofuels: A Case of Non-Governance at the Global Level?" *Global Environmental Politics* 13, no. 2 (2013): 46–64.

66 Carolyn M. Dudek, "Transmitting Environmentalism? The Unintended Global Consequences of European Union Environmental Policies," *Global Environmental Politics* 13, no. 2 (2013): 109–27.

67 European Commission, *Communication from the Commission to the European Parliament, the Council, the European Economic and Social Committee and the Committee of the Regions: Increasing the Impact of EU Development Policy: An Agenda for Change, COM (2011), 637 Final* (2011).

68 See development.donoratlas.eu/infographics/Global%20Trends%20-%20Infographic%20-%202012.pdf.

7 The future of EU environmental governance

- **Maintaining environmental policymaking and improving implementation**
- **Enhancing environmental policy integration and sustainability**
- **Exercising influence beyond the EU borders**

In a world with so much environmental degradation, activism, research and policymaking, and so little progress toward greater sustainability, what is next for EU environmental governance? Certainly, EU legal, political and organizational developments continue apace. Perhaps nowhere is this more clear than in environmental governance, which has been heavily Europeanized over the last two generations. Yet, EU institution building and deepening integration do not follow linear, predetermined paths. Tensions persist between those EU bodies and member states whose leaders, with varying levels of public support, seek greater supranationalism by transferring even more competency to the EU level, and those politicians and voters who prefer to keep many aspects of intergovernmental relations unchanged with national governments and parliaments retaining powers over critical economic and social issues. In these debates, environmental policy and sustainable development issues, on which the EU holds much influence, are often central.[1]

Different theoretical approaches to the study of European integration draw attention to multiple legal, political, economic, and social factors and actors shaping policy developments in the short, medium, and long terms. Intergovernmentalism highlights those instances where environmental goals and policies are decided through high-level negotiations including in the European Council. Neo-functionalism, new institutionalism, and constructivism draw attention, in different ways, to the many processes through which EU bodies, member states, and stakeholder groups advance environmental issues through lower-level political and administrative processes, including the ordinary legislative procedure and the comitology system, and how interests, norms and ideas change over time. Multilevel governance and Europeanization studies explore how environmental policymaking and implementation are growing more connected across administrative levels, and how standards and practices are harmonized across the continent while some structures are more difficult to alter. Adding more complexity, different political actors conceptualize European and global sustainability in varying and sometimes conflicting ways.

The EU's ability to meet the many challenges facing member states and citizens differs considerably across political, economic, and social issue areas where a host of environmental issues demand serious and continuous attention. As environmental governance remains important to future European integration, the environment is among the few major policy areas in which the EU consistently enjoys relatively broad member state support and high public approval ratings among people from different parts of the EU. This chapter summarizes a few critical insights from EU environmental governance and discusses challenges to EU maintenance of its environmental policy influence in the years ahead. It focuses on three sets of issues central to strengthening environmental governance: 1) maintaining environmental policymaking and improving implementation; 2) enhancing environmental policy integration and sustainability; and 3) exercising influence beyond the EU borders.

Maintaining environmental policymaking and improving implementation

Since the 1980s, EU environmental policy has expanded significantly, made possible by a series of treaty amendments affording greater authority to EU bodies. Coupled with substantial membership enlargements and expansions of the single market, EU environmental policy now significantly impacts a larger number of European countries. The EU has massive governance systems on air and water pollution, waste management, hazardous chemicals, GMOs, biodiversity, and climate change. Many laws embody high levels of ambition—their mandates and requirements are among the most extensive and demanding anywhere in the world. Yet, each issue area is plagued by persistent implementation deficits. Agricultural and fisheries policies attract substantial and well-deserved criticism for not achieving basic ecological protection and failing to respond to scientific data. While many environmental policy developments are impressive in both ambition and scope, questions remain regarding whether the EU possesses the political, economic and social capabilities needed to maintain policy momentum and address lingering implementation gaps in both older and newer EU member states?

EU environmental law relies heavily on command-and-control regulations and directives, but market-based instruments and the use of economic incentives are becoming more important in climate change mitigation, waste management, and water policy. Several recent policy developments on, for example, air and water pollution and biodiversity protection also have a strong ecosystem focus. This follows trends in Europe and elsewhere of moving away from early source-specific legislation dating back to the 1960s—mainly setting targets and mandates for individual point sources such as large industrial plants—to taking more effects-based and holistic approaches to environmental governance. Increasingly, EU policy is not simply controlling what comes out of a chimney or a tailpipe, but trying to assess which kinds of more comprehensive regulatory measures are needed to protect ecosystems with varying levels of ecological sensitivity and resilience. As the WFD, the REACH regulation and the Natura 2000 network demonstrate, this may involve major reorganization of governance structures, decision-making processes, and public and private sector behavior.

The 2014 climate and energy agreement and introduction of several major reform packages in 2013 covering air pollution, the CAP, and the CFP, show that environmental policymaking has not come to a standstill, even during difficult economic times. At the same time, EU bodies, member states and interest groups sometimes openly disagree over where and how far they should move. For example, efforts to tighten GHG controls through the ETS led by the European Commission, the European Parliament, some member states, and environmental advocacy groups are met by fierce opposition by other countries and industry interests. While some resistance relates to an unwillingness to give the EU more regulatory authority, much is grounded in financial concerns: proposed measures are seen to be too expensive. Some environmental policy expansions undoubtedly cost money, but reports on, for example, pollution abatement and chemicals management also assess significant human health, environmental and economic efficiency benefits from stricter controls.[2] In addition, a 2011 report estimated that failure to comply with existing legislation resulted in environmental and human health-related costs totaling €50 billion per year.[3]

Major areas of environmental policy continue to rely on effort sharing and preferential treatment of relatively less wealthy member states. Several newer member states have less ambitious national GHG reduction targets than the average EU target for 2020 and they are given special exemptions on the allocation and auctioning of ETS allowances. Member states also have different national reduction goals on other air pollutants, related to their levels of national economic development and the application of critical loads/levels. These kinds of differentiations are helpful in the formulation of collective approaches based on individual national targets and abilities. Yet, some implementation gaps result from of a lack of political will in member states to follow through with diligently transposing and enforcing EU laws. In such instances, European Commission-initiated infringement procedures are time consuming, even if the Court of Justice has been generally supportive of the European Commission's positions in its rulings. In addition, corruption plagues EU co-funded environmental projects in many member states.

It therefore comes as no surprise that recent expansions of environmental policy have mixed implementation records (at best), often with complex and sometimes surprising variations across member states. For example, Denmark and Germany, long considered green leader states supporting stringent national targets and mandates, were the only two member states to exceed three of their four NECs in 2010 (for nitrogen oxide, VOCs, and ammonia), continuing to struggle with implementation and enforcement in 2011.[4] Poland, which is often seen as a laggard not least on climate change based on high GHG emissions from coal use and much recent interest in hydraulic fracturing (or "fracking"), is among a minority of member states to invoke national safety measures on GMOs on environmental and health grounds. In contrast, the UK and Sweden express support for more GMO cultivation and use, while having pushed hard for strict chemicals management, supported ambitious GHG reduction targets, and promoted renewable energy expansions. Some member states have better implementation records and have faced fewer infringement procedures than others, but progress on implementation and enforcement is needed across the board for the EU to continue its environmental leadership.

Enhancing environmental policy integration and sustainability

Even as the EU looks to maintain environmental policymaking momentum and address implementation deficits, clearly it has driven many regional institutional innovations and ecological improvements over the past three decades. Atmospheric and aquatic emissions of many hazardous substances are significantly reduced, more waste is recycled and less is put in landfills, commercial chemicals on the single market are subject to systematic screening and individual controls, more territory is designated for nature and biodiversity protection, GHG emissions are on a downward trajectory, and renewable energy continues to expand—to name a few areas where regional progress is measurable. The EU's ecological footprint compares fairly well when judged against those of other industrialized countries, but it remains large in relation to developing countries and the amount of natural resources available in Europe.[5] Can the EU better integrate environmental concerns into all areas of Union policy and economic activity and make more progress towards member states' societal sustainability?

Despite EU treaty statements that environmental requirements shall be part of all other policy areas, much more effective environmental policy integration is necessary to reduce the Union's ecological footprint. While some recent efforts in several issue areas take a more holistic and ecologically focused governance approach, much environmental policy remains sectoral and limited in scope. For example, the WFD goal of a "good status" for all surface and ground water cannot be achieved by water-specific legislation and the establishment of decentralized river basin-based institutions alone. Fulfilling this goal requires coordinated and substantive policy developments and implementation measures related to waste management, chemicals regulation, farming practices, biodiversity protection, and tourism and recreation. Likewise, goals related to slowing and reversing biodiversity loss cannot be reached without a much more comprehensive approach to air and water pollution control, agricultural and fisheries practices, GMO cultivation, forest management, climate change mitigation and adaptation, transportation, development, and land-use changes.

Policy integration challenges are nowhere more obvious and complex than those related to climate change—a topic elevated to the highest political agendas and one in which the EU touts itself as a frontrunner. Climate change mitigation and adaptation issues connect to a wide range of societal areas, impacting public, private and civil society actors in numerous and far-reaching ways. For the EU to go beyond the 2020 and 2030 GHG reduction goals and achieve substantial reductions by 2050 consistent with the 2°C target, it must accomplish nothing less than an economy-wide transition away from fossil fuels for generating electricity. Yet even this enormous task is not enough; necessary GHG cuts require a restructuring of transportation systems and the formulation of more stringent approaches to forest management and biodiversity protection. European societies are only beginning to address adaptation needs, and design and implement plans to protect critical infrastructure and reduce other climate change-related risks, which vary greatly across geographical locations and societies. Many future adaptation needs may also currently be unknown.

In addition, improved policy integration is integral to advancing the sustainability agenda, of which enhanced climate change mitigation and adaptation is only one part. Many changes to European production and consumption patterns are needed to reduce the EU's natural resource use. So far, sustainable development and ecological modernization efforts by EU bodies and member states fall largely within the sphere of weak sustainability. They take place under EU and state-centric governance structures, as environmental issues and policy have become mainstream in European societies, but lacking severely in terms of effective environmental policy integration. EU policies and programs seek to green economic policy, budgets, and markets under the largely unchanged political framework of capitalist exchange and free trade that continue to constitute the core of the single market. EU documents, plans and funds focus attention on issues of social cohesion, seeking to reduce socioeconomic differences across member states, but without challenging existing economic practices and institutions at a deeper level.

To critics, however, the EU merely engages in the politics of institutionalizing unsustainability.[6] They argue that the shift to a post-carbon economy requires fundamental change in states, markets, and communities, and that efforts to create a green economy—largely greening "business as usual"—are fundamentally insufficient. From this more radical perspective, political, economic and cultural causes of existing unsustainability—the exploitation of people and the planet—must be thoroughly transformed before societies can hope to achieve sustainability. They seek to replace orthodox notions of economic productivity with alternative concepts such as that of "human flourishing," whereby socioeconomic inequality is deeply addressed and humans thrive while energy and natural resource use stay within the boundaries of an ecologically finite planet. Such critiques focus on sufficiency and human well-being as an alternative to neoclassical definitions of economic growth and consumption-led prosperity. For some social theorists, the transition to such a world is not only inevitable and necessary, but highly desirable.[7]

Exercising influence beyond the EU borders

The EU is an ubiquitous actor on the international stage, having explicit leadership aspirations. EU bodies, member states and others who favor a more federalist EU are often unhappy with the Union's frequent inability to act uniformly and effectively across major foreign policy areas, despite the recent creation of a High Representative of the Union for Foreign Affairs and Security Policy and the EEAS. In contrast, those in Europe who are skeptical of affording the EU greater foreign policy competence seek to maintain current limitations on EU bodies' abilities to make foreign policy decisions on behalf of all member states. However, in international trade and environmental politics the EU has achieved a relatively high degree of uniformity in its contact with others. These issues are central to EU efforts to expand the Union's role in international politics more generally. Yet, can the EU continue to assert influence in external relations and not only shape international environmental and sustainability agendas but also directly impact negotiated policy outcomes?

The EU—the only regional organization independently engaging international affairs including as a separate party to multilateral treaties—faces important challenges in global forums. Its soft power approach and leadership ambitions are perhaps most tested in the climate change area. The EU's long-standing support for a legally binding approach failed to generate necessary support from countries in Copenhagen in 2009.[8] With a current focus on a post-2020 global climate change agreement, industrialized countries including the United States, Canada, Russia, and Australia remain reluctant, especially opposing any legally binding agreement based on the principle of common but differentiated responsibility that requires few significant commitments from China, India and other emerging economies, which in turn, resist calls to take on clear national reduction targets. Furthermore, while the European Commission, the European Parliament and many environmental groups back tougher internal measures and more ambitious targets helping to underpin the EU's external position, member states and industry representatives express very different levels of support for these measures.

The EU is a key party in tough negotiations on issues such as addressing acidification and eutrophication under CLRTAP, the control of additional chemicals under the Stockholm and Rotterdam Conventions, deadlines for the phasing out of specific classes of ozone-depleting substances under the Montreal Protocol, and measures for addressing mercury pollution from coal-fired power plants under the Minamata Convention. Initiatives under these and other treaties are important to address activities in other countries that impact ecological and human health conditions in Europe. While EU policy in many of these areas is consistent with, or ahead of, global commitments, internal challenges to meeting goals in areas such as biodiversity protection, agriculture and fisheries management are much greater. In multilateral forums the EU and member states also face demands for greater financial support for developing countries. In addition, the European Commission and member states play key roles in regional environmental agreements whose implementation often has direct consequences for ecological conditions within the EU.

Through the EEAS and the European Commission, the EU seeks to expand its multilateral and bilateral relationships using combinations of soft power and soft imperialism approaches. The EU engages prospective member states and others in the neighborhood with overt expectations that these countries should shift towards EU norms and standards, rather than the other way round. The promise of full membership is a very valuable carrot, influencing countries actively seeking it. Deepening political and economic connections, including greater access to the single market, can also be attractive for countries not looking for (or not eligible for) membership, but generally less influential than membership prospects. In these external relationships, environmental and sustainable development issues often come in behind broader governance and economic issues (e.g. democracy, human rights, free markets, etc.), but they remain explicitly part of a large number of political processes and legal agreements. Many are also coupled with financial support for environment and sustainable development projects in other countries.

As the number of international environmental and free trade agreements continues to grow, the two sets of issues become more intertwined. Such connections are actively pushed by EU officials, becoming an increasingly important way in which the EU exercises influence on environment and sustainable development in external relations. Trade-related negotiations, however, can be contentious. They can deepen connections with long-standing allies such as the United States, Canada and Japan, even as they illustrate that leading industrialized countries have differing values and interests around issues such as GMOs and climate change. The increase in trade and investment agreements also illustrates the EU's growing political and economic cooperation with China, India, Brazil and other emerging powers, whose firms are increasingly competing with European businesses in European and global markets. In the coming decades, European policies, states, firms, activists and consumers will continue to impact European and global ecological conditions and sustainability efforts, affecting the lives of billions of people around the world. If the EU is to play an important role in engendering greater global environmental protection and sustainability, it will need to achieve its goals and meet its challenges at home, and enhance its influence abroad.

Notes

1 Henrik Selin and Stacy D. VanDeveer, "EU Environmental Politics, Policies, and Results, " *Annual Review of Environment and Resources*, forthcoming 2015.
2 European Environment Agency, *Air Quality in Europe—2013 Report* (Copenhagen, 2013); European Commission, *Questions and Answers on the EU Clean Air Package* (Brussels, 18 December 2013); Antonia Reihlen and Heike Lüskow, *Analysis of Studies Discussing Benefits of REACH* (Hamburg: Ökopol Institut für Ökologie und Politik GmbH, 2007).
3 European Commission, *The Costs of Not Implementing the Environmental Acquis* (Brussels, 2012).
4 European Environment Agency, *Report No. 6/2013 NEC Directive Status Report 2012: EEA Technical Report* (Copenhagen, 2013).
5 European Environment Agency, *The European Environment—State and Outlook 2010* (Copenhagen, 2010).
6 Hayley Stevenson, *Institutionalizing Unsustainability: The Paradox of Global Climate Governance* (Berkeley, Calif.: California University Press, 2012).
7 John Barry, *The Politics of Actually Existing Unsustainability: Human Flourishing in a Climate-Changed, Carbon-Constrained World* (Oxford: Oxford University Press, 2012).
8 Radoslav Dimitrov, "Inside UN Climate Change Negotiations: The Copenhagen Conference," *Review of Policy Research* 27, no. 6 (2010): 795–821.

Select Bibliography

Tanja A. Börzel, "Pace-Setting, Foot-dragging and Fence-sitting: Member State Responses to Europeanization," *Journal of Common Market Studies* 40, no. 2 (2002): 193–214. Discusses different member state responses to and strategies toward environmental regulation in the EU.

JoAnn Carmin and Stacy D. VanDeveer, eds, *EU Enlargement and the Environment: Institutional Change and Environmental Policy in Central and Eastern Europe* (New York: Routledge, 2005). Assesses the impacts of joining the EU in Central and Eastern European countries.

Tom Delreux, *The EU as International Environmental Negotiator* (Aldershot: Ashgate, 2011). Explores the role of the EU in international environmental cooperation and treaty making.

Noelle Eckley and Henrik Selin, "All Talk, Little Action: Precaution and its Effects on European Chemicals Regulation," *Journal of European Public Policy* 11, no. 1 (2004): 78–105. Discusses efforts to implement the precautionary principle in EU environmental regulation.

Liesbet Hooghe and Gary Marks, *Multi-Level Governance and European Integration* (Lanham, Md.: Rowman and Littlefield, 2001). Draws from the early literature on multi-level governance as originally applied to the study of the EU.

Andrew J. Jordan and Andrea Lenschow, eds, *Innovation in Environmental Policy? Integrating the Environment for Sustainability* (Northampton, Mass.: Edward Elgar, 2008). Discusses challenges to environmental policy integration within the EU.

Andrew Jordan and Duncan Liefferink, eds, *Environmental Policy in Europe: The Europeanization of National Environmental Policy* (New York: Routledge, 2005). Analyzes how different member states are impacted by the growing body of EU environmental law.

Mark A. Pollack and Gregory C. Shaffer, *When Cooperation Fails: The International Law and Politics of Genetically Modified Foods* (Oxford: Oxford University Press, 2009). Examines European, transatlantic and international policymaking and politics around GMOs.

Rüdiger K.W. Wurzel, Anthony R. Zito, and Andrew J. Jordan, *Environmental Governance in Europe: A Comparative Analysis of New Environmental Policy Instruments* (Northampton, Mass.: Edward Elgar, 2013). Examines the use of different kinds of policy instruments in the EU and member states.

Derek W. Urwin, *The Community of Europe: A History of European Integration since 1945*, second edn (Harlow: Pearson Education, 1995). Provides a major overview of the development of the EU since the early days of modern European integration.

David Vogel, *The Politics of Precaution: Regulating Health, Safety, and Environmental Risks in Europe and the United States* (Princeton, N.J.: Princeton University Press, 2012). Comparative study of policy divergence in environmental regulations in the EU and the United States.

Helen Wallace, Mark A. Pollack and Alasdair R. Young, eds, *Policy-Making in the European Union* (Oxford: Oxford University Press, 2010). Comprehensive examination of actors and processes of decision making within the EU.

Albert Weale, Geoffrey Pridham, Michelle Cini, Dimitrios Konstadakopulos, Martin Porter, and Brendan Flynn, *Environmental Governance in Europe: An Ever Closer Ecological Union?* (Oxford: Oxford University Press, 2000). Analysis and much empirical information about the early phase of EU environmental policymaking.

Internet sources

Council of the European Union (www.consilium.europa.eu): Information about how member states work together and engage in collective decision making across different issue areas.

Court of Justice (curia.europa.eu): Information about the activities of the Court of Justice and recent and past opinions and judgments on cases relating to European integration and the workings of the EU.

European Commission (ec.europa.eu): Information about the role of the European Commission, how its work is divided into different DGs and Services, and summaries of EU legislation.

European Council (www.european-council.europa.eu): Information about the regular high-level meeting of the political leaders of member states setting agendas and discussing high-profile issues.

European Environment Agency (www.eea.europa.eu): Provides reports and scientific data on environmental issues and ecological trends in individual member states and the EU as a whole.

European Environment Bureau (www.eeb.org): Outlines major concerns and activities of environmental advocacy groups active on the EU level as well as in individual member states.

European Parliament (www.europarl.europa.eu): Information about the operations of the European Parliament, its committees, and its role in the ordinary legislative procedure.

Index

Adenauer, Konrad 30
African Union 119, 138
agriculture and rural development
103; DG Agriculture and Rural
Development 54, 75; EU budget
103, 104; infringement procedure
84; organic production 105;
SAPARD 134; sustainable
development 103; *see also* CAP
air pollution policy 90–2, 130, 147;
2005 Thematic Strategy on Air
Pollution 90; 2013 Clean Air
Policy Package 90, 91; air
pollutants 90; mandating national
emission reductions 90, 91–2;
NEC 91, 92, 149; regulating
specific sources and sectors 90, 92;
setting air quality standards 90–1;
seventh EAP 90; shortcomings:
failure to achieve emission
reduction goals 10, 92; success:
reduction of emissions of air
pollutants 9, 92, 149; transboundary problems 8; *see also* carbon
dioxide; CLRTAP; GHG
Albania 5, 59, 132
American Chamber of Commerce 62
American Chemistry Council 62–3
ammonia 9, 91, 149
Amsterdam Treaty 3, 33, 43–4, 46
Andreotti, Giulio 34
Australia 110, 152
Austria 31, 92, 98, 112, 113; EU
membership 42, 131; GMO 101,
102

Basel Convention 95, 124, 125, 136
Belgium 92, 95, 113; EU founding
member 30–1
biodiversity 7, 90, 108–110, 125,
130, 147; 1992 Convention on
Biological Diversity 101; biodiversity loss 10, 108, 121; Biodiversity Strategy 108–110; CAP
109; CFP 109; climate change
108, 110; drivers of biodiversity
loss 108; GMO standards 110;
Natura 2000 network 109, 110, 130,
148; shortcomings 10, 108, 110, 113,
121, 152; success 110, 150
Borg, Joe 107
Brandt, Willy 34
Brundtland Report 36, 46
BusinessEurope 61

cadmium 8, 91, 115
Canada 136; EU/Canada free trade
agreement 136; transatlantic relations and environmental policy
135–8
CAP (Common Agricultural Policy)
31, 90, 103–105; biodiversity 109;
controversial issue 103–105; criticism 104–105, 147; EEC 104;
lobbying 61; organic production
105; priorities 103 (balanced
development of rural areas 103;
sustainable management of
natural resources 103; viable food
production 103); Rome Treaty
104; shortcomings 113, 147, 152;

De Gaulle, Charles 31
democracy 43; EU democratic
legitimacy 13, 86; EU membership and democracy 4, 38, 131–2;
Norway, 'fax democracy' 43;
PHARE 134; soft power 120
Denmark 2, 149; bottle recycling
scheme 96; leadership role on
environmental issues 42, 149;
waste management 96
developing country 110, 126, 139,
140, 150, 153

EAP (Environmental Action Programme) 7, 34–5, 36–7, 127; 1st
EAP 35, 36, 72, 73, 127; 4th EAP
36, 40, 81; 5th EAP 36, 40, 42;
6th EAP 37, 45, 98; 7th EAP 37,
45, 90; Council of the European
Union 35; EEC, 1972 Paris
summit 34; formal legal act 41;
sustainability 36, 45, 46
EC (European Community) 39, 40,
41, 120
ECB (European Central Bank) 51, 57
ECHA (European Chemicals
Agency) 59, 99, 100
eco-labeling 65, 66; organic labeling
105
ecological modernization 23, 25–6,
47, 68
economics: chemicals management
and economic growth 100; costs
from failure to comply with
environmental policies 148; economic growth and the environment
97, 100, 151; environment/
economics connection 23–4, 25,
151; environmental policy costs
148; environmental protection and
continued economic growth 25; EU
economic diversity 6; green
economy 25, 151; *see also* EU
budget
ECSC (European Coal and Steel
Community) 16, 30, 32, 39, 41
EEA (European Environment
Agency) 59, 75, 81, 82; State of
the European Environment
reports 9, 10, 26, 59, 81

EEAS (European External Action
Service 52, 119, 132, 133, 135,
152, 153; EU's diplomatic arm 43,
49, 118
EEB (European Environmental
Bureau) 62
EEC (European Economic Community) 2, 13, 31, 119; 1972 Paris
summit 34; CAP 104; environmental issues 4, 34, 35, 120;
environmental protection as an
essential EEC objective 37–8;
SEA 39, 120; UK 31; *see also*
Rome Treaty
EFCA (European Fisheries Control
Agency) 59–60, 106, 107
effort/burden sharing principle 72,
73–4, 111, 148
EFSA (European Food Safety
Authority) 59, 102, 105
EFTA (European Free Trade Association) 3, 31, 38, 89, 98, 132,
138; EU/EFTA relationship 42–3;
European Economic Area treaty
42–3; Europeanization of, and
diplomacy/democracy conflict 43
Einstein, Albert 1
energy: 2009 Climate and Energy
Package: '20–20–20' goals 111;
DG Energy 54; energy efficiency 68,
111, 112, 113; energy performance
84; infringement procedure 84;
nuclear energy 112–13; sustainability 7; *see also* renewable
energy
enforcement 81–6, 149; CAP 107;
Court of Justice 38, 41, 83–4;
European Commission 38, 53, 82
(infringement procedure 82–4);
financial penalty 38, 41, 67, 83,
84; inadequate enforcement of EU
environmental legislation 46; *see
also* environmental policy
implementation
ENP (European Neighbourhood
Policy) 133, 134, 135, 139
environmental governance 6–9, 89–
90; complexity 7, 97, 113–14, 146;
decision making 7; environmental
protection as core goal of the

Routledge Global Institutions Series

6 Global Environmental Institutions (2006)
by Elizabeth R. DeSombre (Wellesley College)

5 Internal Displacement (2006)
Conceptualization and its consequences
by Thomas G. Weiss (The CUNY Graduate Center) and David A. Korn

4 The UN General Assembly (2005)
by M. J. Peterson (University of Massachusetts, Amherst)

3 United Nations Global Conferences (2005)
by Michael G. Schechter (Michigan State University)

2 The UN Secretary-General and Secretariat (2005)
by Leon Gordenker (Princeton University)

1 The United Nations and Human Rights (2005)
A guide for a new era
by Julie A. Mertus (American University)

Books currently under contract include:

The Regional Development Banks
Lending with a regional flavor
by Jonathan R. Strand (University of Nevada)

Millennium Development Goals (MDGs)
For a people-centered development agenda?
by Sakiko Fukada-Parr (The New School)

The Bank for International Settlements
The politics of global financial supervision in the age of high finance
by Kevin Ozgercin (SUNY College at Old Westbury)

International Migration
by Khalid Koser (Geneva Centre for Security Policy)

Human Development
by Richard Ponzio

The International Monetary Fund (2nd edition)
Politics of conditional lending
by James Raymond Vreeland (Georgetown University)

The UN Global Compact
by Catia Gregoratti (Lund University)

Institutions for Women's Rights
by Charlotte Patton (York College, CUNY) and
Carolyn Stephenson (University of Hawaii)

International Aid
by Paul Mosley (University of Sheffield)

Global Consumer Policy
by Karsten Ronit (University of Copenhagen)

The Changing Political Map of Global Governance
by Anthony Payne (University of Sheffield) and
Stephen Robert Buzdugan (Manchester Metropolitan University)

Coping with Nuclear Weapons
by W. Pal Sidhu

Global Governance and China
The dragon's learning curve
edited by Scott Kennedy (Indiana University)

The Politics of Global Economic Surveillance
by Martin S. Edwards (Seton Hall University)

Mercy and Mercenaries
Humanitarian agencies and private security companies
by Peter Hoffman

Regional Organizations in the Middle East
by James Worrall (University of Leeds)

Reforming the UN Development System
The Politics of Incrementalism
by Silke Weinlich (Duisburg-Essen University)

The United Nations as a Knowledge Organization
by Nanette Svenson (Tulane University)

The International Criminal Court
The Politics and practice of prosecuting atrocity crimes
by Martin Mennecke (University of Copenhagen)

The Politics of International Organizations
Views from insiders
edited by Patrick Weller (Griffith University) and
Xu Yi-chong (Griffith University)

The African Union (2nd edition)
Challenges of globalization, security, and governance
by Samuel M. Makinda (Murdoch University),
F. Wafula Okumu (African Union), and
David Mickler (University of Western Australia)

BRICS
by João Pontes Nogueira (Catholic University, Rio de Janeiro) and
Monica Herz (Catholic University, Rio de Janeiro)

Expert Knowledge in Global Trade
edited by Erin Hannah (University of Western Ontario),
James Scott (University of Manchester), and
Silke Trommer (Murdoch University)

The European Union (2nd edition)
Clive Archer (Manchester Metropolitan University)

Governing Climate Change (2nd edition)
Peter Newell (University of East Anglia) and
Harriet A. Bulkeley (Durham University)

Contemporary Human Rights Ideas (2nd edition)
Betrand Ramcharan (Geneva Graduate Institute of
International and Development Studies)

Protecting the Internally Displaced
Rhetoric and reality
Phil Orchard (University of Queensland)

The Arctic Council
Within the far north
Douglas C. Nord (Umea University)

For further information regarding the series, please contact:

Nicola Parkin, Editor, Politics & International Studies
Taylor & Francis
2 Park Square, Milton Park, Abingdon
Oxford OX14 4RN, UK
Nicola.parkin@tandf.co.uk
www.routledge.com

9 780415 628822